CONTENTS

FOREWORD

I have a conviction that in these easygoing days, spiritually, we ought to preach more sermons on the great fundamental doctrines of the Christian faith.

At the same time, however, we must couch these messages in the simplest terms possible so that the average layman in the pew can understand these doctrines. I have tried to reach this ideal in the simple sermons in this book.

I am grateful to my faithful secretary, Miss Eva L. Gass, for her help, and to that matchless minister of Christ, Dr. Robert G. Lee, for writing the Introduction.

I hope that these sermons may be used of God to bless many hearts. My preacher brethren are certainly free to use these messages in any way that will help them to "adorn the doctrine of God our Saviour" (Titus 2:10).

W. HERSCHEL FORD

Simple Sermons on Great Christian Doctrines

W. Herschel Ford

BAKER BOOK HOUSE
Grand Rapids, Michigan 49506

ISBN: 0-8010-3519-8

Fifth printing, April 1990

Printed in the United
States of America

INTRODUCTION

In the sixth chapter of John's Gospel, we find Jesus piling doctrinal stones one upon another. In that chapter we have the teaching of the incarnation, the deity of Jesus, redemption by Christ's blood, forgiveness of sins, divine revelation, resurrection, ascension. Following the example of Jesus, writing as a man of God, and possessing wisdom from above, Dr. Ford, in his new book, SIMPLE SERMONS ON THE GREAT CHRISTIAN DOCTRINES, has fashioned into a beautiful temple of truth great doctrinal stones. He has rendered a superlative ministry in setting forth in words of profound simplicity doctrinal truths which every preacher, teacher, and Christian should know and make known to others—truths about God, Christ, the Holy Spirit, Satan, sin, regeneration, atonement through Christ's blood, sanctification, justification by faith, the second coming of Christ, hell, heaven.

To me each chapter is unquestionably a classic—deserving universal reading, meriting highest commendation for its interpretation *of* and loyalty *to* God's sovereign Word. There is profitable preaching ground as well as doctrinal material for all the preachers in the land for months of preaching. Wonderful would be the enrichment in knowledge of our great Christian doctrines in the lives of all our people if they would read and study these masterful sermons. Such knowledge is greatly to be desired.

Spiritual illumination and soundness in the faith once delivered would be the result if these sermons were preached, taught, read, acted upon. As old Ben Franklin advised young men to study the Bible, so I advise people to get this book and become familiar with the enriching contents of Dr. Ford's book.

I do not see how any preacher who knows of this book can afford to be without it, because it sets forth our great Christian doctrines with a devoutly-to-be-desired and wise simplicity which makes all who read the contents the beneficiaries of the author's straight thinking and usage of words. So long as this book is printed, there is no excuse for any Christian being ignorant of or having only a partial knowledge of the great Christian doctrines. This book deserves to be the favorite rendezvous of all who avoid the faintly-outlined road to a palace of truth.

This book by Dr. Ford will prove to be invaluable to Southern Baptists at this time when we are more effectively to familiarize our people with our great Baptist doctrines.

ROBERT G. LEE

1

WHAT KIND OF BEING IS GOD?

The heavens declare the glory of God; and the firmament sheweth his handywork.—PSALM 19:1.

The fool hath said in his heart, There is no God.—PSALM 14:1.

Only a fool would say, "There is no God." When David lifted up his eyes and looked upon all the glories and beauties of the universe, there is no wonder that he burst forth into a psalm of praise to God, the Author and Creator of it all. We preach from the assumption that there is a God, that he has existed from the timeless past and will exist for all eternity. "In the beginning God created the heaven and the earth." He will still exist when the heaven and the earth are no more. A human author doesn't try to prove his own existence—he simply stamps his name on his book and sends it out into the world. And so it is that God has stamped his name upon the first page of the Bible, and all the way through it we must recognize his existence.

Down through all the ages men have wanted to know what kind of being God is. They have said, "Shew us the Father, and it sufficeth us." They want to know how God looks and how he feels toward men and what his attributes are. The Bible reveals God, but this is not the best revelation. Nature reveals God, but this is not a complete revelation. Jesus Christ himself is the one and only complete revelation of the Heavenly Father. He said, "He that hath seen me hath seen the Father." Jesus showed in his life the kind of being that God is. Let us look deeply into this great doctrine of God.

I. The Personality of God

1. He Is a Spirit

John 4:24 says, "God is a Spirit: and they that worship him must worship him in spirit and in truth." This verse means that, although God is very real, he is not material and not visible to us. He met Moses upon the mountaintop, and Moses cried out, "Shew me thy glory." God replied to him, "I will make all my goodness to pass before thee," but "thou canst not see my face."

If God is real, he must have a form. Did he not say, "Let us make man in our own image"? and yet it is not a physical form but a spiritual form. We shall never look upon that form in this world, but we shall see him in all his glory in heaven when we, too, have been given a spiritual existence like unto him. When Stephen was being stoned, he declared, "I see Jesus standing at the right hand of God." He must have seen God in his spiritual form. God moves in his Spirit through the world and we do not see him, but in heaven we shall see him face to face.

2. He Is a Person

He knows, he feels, he loves, he hears prayers, he speaks, he acts. The Bible always represents him as a person, as a living God. He is a free person; he is not bound by any limitations, but he can act free as he pleases with his power. He is unhampered and unlimited in his power. He is highest above all and mightiest over all. He is the author of universal order in matter, life, and mind. Such an order as this could come only from infinite intelligence. When we look upon this old world with all its wonders—when we think of the regularity of night and day, when we think of the constancy of the seasons, when we think of the faithfulness of the sun, the moon, and the stars, when we think about the wonderful machine which is man, we cannot help but say, "Thy wisdom is above the wisdom of the wisest of men; thy thoughts are as high above our thoughts as the heaven is above the earth."

II. THE ATTRIBUTES OF GOD

1. God Is Holy

The Bible labors through many types, sacrifices, and ceremonies to bring out the fact that God is holy. The prophet describes him as "the high and lofty One that inhabiteth eternity, whose name is Holy." As he sits upon the Revelation throne, the angels sing out, "Holy, holy, holy, Lord God Almighty!" Jesus taught us that God is holy—the only holy One.

In a vision Isaiah saw God lifted up upon his throne. He heard the seraphims crying out, "Holy, holy, holy, is the Lord of hosts." When Isaiah saw God and heard these words, even though he was the best man of his day, he hid his face, and cried out, "Woe is me! for I am undone; because I am a man of unclean lips." Although he was a good man, although he was God's servant, he was so overwhelmed by the holiness of God that he felt himself unclean in his presence. If we could catch a real vision of the holiness of God today, we would all cry out, "Unclean! Unclean!"

2. God Is Eternal

The heavens and earth have been here for a long time, but God was here before their time. He was here before "the morning stars sang together, and all the sons of God shouted for joy." It has been a long time since Columbus discovered America, but that is a short time compared with the life of God. A museum in Cairo contains the mummified body of one of the Pharaohs who reigned about the time of Moses. If this man were alive today, his life would be short compared with that of God.

We think of the crude life of our first parents, Adam and Eve, and all the many changes which have come into the world since that time; but God was before it all. Go back into the timeless past where no stars ever shine and no seraphs ever sing, and you will still be in the presence of God. He is the great I Am to whom a thousand years are as but a day. Before the mountains were brought forth, he was; and after the earth is crumbled into the dust, he will still live. He always was, he always is, and he always will be. Yes, God is eternal.

3. God Is Omnipotent

That is, he is all-powerful. Pharaoh thought he was a mighty ruler. Napoleon and the Kaiser and Hitler thought they were mighty monarchs, but all the powers of the earth must bow down before the great God. The winds and waves obey his will—he speaks, and it is done. Jesus said, "With God all things are possible." Jeremiah 32:17: "Ah Lord God! behold, thou hast made the heaven and the earth by thy great power and stretched out arm, and there is nothing too hard for thee." Job 42:2: "I know that thou canst do every thing."

When God was making the world, he said, "Let there be light," and in less than a second's time light was flooding the universe. By a simple utterance God brings to pass that which he wants to happen because all power is his. Not only is nature subservient to him, but man is also subject to his will. James tells us that we are not to say, "I will do thus and so tomorrow," but we will do these things if the Lord wills. Happy is the man who subjects himself to the will of God, but whether he does this or not, he is subject to him. He is greater than all rulers and will carry out his eternal purpose in our lives and in the world.

4. God Is Omniscient

Because God is omniscient, he knows all things. John 3:20: "God knoweth all things." Psalm 147:4: "He telleth the number of the stars; he calleth them all by their names." Matthew 10:29: "Are not two sparrows sold for a farthing? and one of them shall not fall on the ground without your Father." God looks down through the ages and takes even the acts of wicked men and makes them work out for our good and for his glory. We have just gone through a great war with all its bloodshed, atrocities, and sorrow, but God knew all about it and will work it out all right. He takes the shocking things of our lives and proves to us that "all things work together for good to them that love God." There are no afterthoughts with God—he knows from all time past what is happening and what will happen on through eternity. He is omniscient.

5. God Is Omnipresent

This means that God is everywhere at all times. Acts 17:27: "He [is] not far from every one of us." He is with us in the brightness of midday and in the blackness of midnight. He was with our boys on the sands of Africa, in the mountains of Germany, and on the barren isles of the Pacific. He is as close to us by sea as by land. He is with us when we are serving him. He is by our side when we go down into sin. If we stop and think and remember that God is there, and that we must account to him, we will be more careful about our daily lives. When you are in sorrow and think that the world has forsaken you, God is there. When troubles like the waves of the sea sweep over your soul, he is still there. He is not a God who is far off.

The heathen tramp many miles to bow down and worship their gods of wood. Our Catholic friends feel that they must be before an altar in a church before they can worship God, or must be in the privacy of a confession box before they can confess their sins. But, my friends, God is anywhere and everywhere when men need him.

6. God Is Great

(1) *He is great in creative power.*—If you want to see the greatness of God, look around you. Look upon the mountains, the rivers, and the oceans. The poet wisely says, "Only God can make a tree." Only a great God can make all the wonderful things which are in the world of nature today. We think of the earth as being very great, but if the sun were hollow, and if you could bore a hole into its surface, you could put a million four hundred thousand worlds in the sun and they would still have room to rattle around. And yet there are many other planets in God's system much larger than the earth. One great God made them all. Let man stand in reverence before him.

When we think of man with his power to think and to plan and to act, we realize that he is the greatest piece of machinery in the world. But God made him with a thought and a word. An infidel once cried out before a large crowd, "If there is a God, let him strike me dead at this minute." God paid no more attention to him than would the mighty ocean to a barking dog. It is foolish for a little man to defy a great God.

(2) *He is great in redemptive power.*—Man was made in innocence, but he sank down into sin. Yet God in mighty redemptive power saves him from his sin. God

made him, the devil unmade him, and God can remake him.

You think of the life of some terrible character, and you say, "Nothing can change that man but God." And God does. You hear of an evangelist who advertises the story of his life with such a title as "From Gambling Den to the Pulpit." What made such a change in his life? Only the redemptive power of a great God. If you are the vilest sinner in all the world, you are the one whom God wants. His power can make your life over for you.

> What a wonderful change in my life has
>   been wrought
> Since Jesus came into my heart!
> I have light in my soul for which long I had
>   sought,
> Since Jesus came into my heart!

(3) *He is great in keeping power.*—When God saves a man, there is no power in earth, heaven, or hell great enough to tear him out of the Father's hand. God is greater than the devil and all the demons of hell. They may assail the soul of man, but God will keep him safe. Jesus said, "They shall never perish, neither shall any man pluck them out of my hand. My Father, which gave them me, is greater than all; and no man is able to pluck them out of my Father's hand." A man may say he cannot hold out. But it is not up to him to hold out; it is up to God. We must fully trust him and not try to live in our own strength. God is great, and all the devils of hell are small compared to him. If we surrender our lives to him, he will keep us safe forever.

7. God Is Loving

Some people think that God is a hard-faced tyrant who looks with displeasure upon a smile, who sends us to hell when we do not toe the mark. This is absolutely wrong. God loves us and God cares for us. If we are punished for our sin, it is not God's fault; it is our fault.

(1) *God's love is shown in the gift of his Son to die for us.*—The greatest love in all the world is not the love of a mother for her child, nor the love of a patriot for his country, but the love of God for lost sinners. Suppose someone should say to me, "You must give up your son that he might die for another man's sin." I would immediately say, "No, I will not sacrifice my son; let the man die in his sin." But what did God say? His Son was the fairest among ten thousand, and the One altogether lovely. God loved him with all his heart, but when he heard the cry of a sin-sick world, he gave his only begotten Son to die that sinners might find the way home to heaven.

Sacrifice is the greatest test of love. A man may tell me that he loves me, but I do not really know that he loves me until he proves it by sacrifice. I read that God loves me, and I believe it, but my faith turns to reality when I come to the cross. I look upon the form of that One who is dying, and I cry out, "Lord, lovest thou me?" And then he shows me the prints of the nails in his hands and in his feet, and I know that God loves me, a sinner. Christ suffered intensely upon the cross, but yonder in heaven God also suffered. Every pang, every groan, and every stripe was a blow to the great heart of the Heavenly Father.

Suppose that one of your sons had been captured by the enemy during the war. Suppose that you had been forced to stand aside and look on while they tortured your son and finally put him to death. It would have hurt you and would have broken your heart. You could never be the same again. But let me tell you that God looked on when sin put his only begotten Son to death. It hurt the great heart of God, but he bore it all because of his mighty love for you and me.

(2) *His love is shown in his daily care.*—We are prone to forget that it is God who cares for us every second of the day. We would have gone down long ago if he hadn't cared for us. We can truly say with Jeremiah of old, "The Lord's mercies . . . are new every morning." When the doctor stands beside the operating table and performs a delicate operation, the slightest slip of his hand might cause death. But God guides that hand. Hundreds of times we have been in a position where one misstep would have meant death. We did not know it, but God was there caring for us.

(3) *God's love is shown in his mercy toward sinners.*— You and I were such wretched sinners that we deserved death, and nothing but death. How God must have loved us to show mercy upon us, even while we were in our sins!

The old Moody Tabernacle in Chicago had these three simple words written above the gas jets over the pulpit, "God Loves You." One day a sinful man came down the street, paused for just a moment and looked into the church. When he saw that sign, he cursed and said, "God doesn't love a rotten man like I am." He went on down the street, but he could not get away from those three words. He was impressed that he ought to go back to the church. He did go back to the church, and walked down the aisle with his eyes fixed upon those words. It happened that just at that time Mr. Moody was coming into the church through another door. He saw the man, talked to him and prayed with him, and soon the man was rejoicing in his salvation. Oh, if we could get men to realize how much God loves them, we could more easily win them to Christ!

III. The Present Relation of God to the World and to Man

1. He Governs the Affairs of the World

At times it seems that the world is tottering upon the brink of disaster, but behind the clouds God is still upon his throne and God is still reigning over the universe. He lifts up nations and casts them down according to his own great purpose. He lifted up many nations in ancient days—these nations went astray in sin and godlessness and the Lord cast them down. He has truly blessed America and given her great privileges and opportunities. If America fails to take advantage of her opportunities, if she continues her headlong way into sin and godlessness, surely the Lord will cast America down.

2. He Punishes Sin and Rewards Righteousness Here upon the Earth

Men cannot break God's laws upon this earth and get away with it. You can say, "Regardless of what the Bible teaches, I will do as I please," but you cannot get away with it. God has some unchangeable laws in this world, and if these laws are broken, punishment automatically comes upon the lawbreaker.

The Christian is punished in this way. A child of God shall never suffer in the world to come, but if he doesn't live as he should in this world, God will chasten him. God's children are also rewarded in this world. If you live a consecrated life and walk according to the will of God, he will bless you here as well as hereafter.

IV. The Future Relation of God to the World and to Man

1. He Will Be a Just Judge

He will judge those who are out of Christ. The rich man, the poor man, the beggar, the thief, the scholar, the dullard, the king, the slave, the great, the small—all men must give an account to God of the way they have lived in this world.

According to God's Word there are two judgment thrones waiting for us out yonder in the future. The first throne will be the judgment seat of Christ where the Lord Jesus will judge all Christians according to their works and reward them in proportion to the way they have served the Lord and lived for his glory. The other throne is the great white throne where Christ shall judge all unbelievers and sinners and punish them according to their works. You will not be able to plead "not guilty" when you stand before that throne. God has a record, and he knows all about everything we have ever done, said, or thought. He offers to save you now; he will be your judge then. His arms are open in a longing, loving invitation now; in that day he will point lost men to an everlasting hell.

2. He will Reward the Faithful and Punish the Sinful

At the judgment seat of Christ he will reward the faithful; at the great white throne he will pronounce punishment upon the sinful. You can get away with your wrong living here, but you will be punished there. You cannot escape the judgment. The hand that was pierced upon the cross for you will point your way into the bottomless pits. But, thank God, those who have trusted Christ are saved now, and they shall be rewarded then.

A minister dreamed that he died and stood before the judgment bar. The question was asked of him, "Have you always been good?" "No," he replied. "Have you always been just?" "No," he replied. "Have you always been pure?" "No," he replied, and he bowed his head for the condemnation which he felt would fall upon him. Then he said a bright light shone about him, and he looked up into the face of Jesus Christ. The Saviour put his arms around him and looked up to the throne and said: "Father, I know he hasn't always been good—he hasn't always been just—he hasn't always been pure; but down there in the world he stood for me, and now I will stand for him here." Thank God, if we confess him here, he will confess us before the Father. In that land of no tears he will give us a bountiful reward. We will lay down the cross and take up the crown.

3. He Will Live Forever with His Children

The greatest joy that can come to a Christian in this world is to have a few minutes of unbroken fellowship with the Heavenly Father. But in heaven we shall have perfect communion with him, "where congregations never break up and sabbaths never end." "Thus shall we ever be with the Lord."

My friends, this is the kind of a God you must live for. He is the kind of God you must meet some day. He is great and good and loving and merciful. He offers his best to you here, but if you reject his offers, he will be your Judge in that other world. Are you ready for that day? Are you ready to meet God and give him an account of your life?

Dr. J. Wilbur Chapman was pastor of a great church in Philadelphia. One morning after the service, one of his church officers said to him: "Dr. Chapman, I wish that you could enjoy the health that I do. I never have an ache or a pain. I never need a doctor, and I never take medicine." Three weeks later Dr. Chapman's phone rang early one morning. He was being called to the home of the church officer. When he arrived at the home, the man's daughter met him at the door. She was sobbing as if her heart would break. She said: "This morning my father waked me and asked me to meet him in the breakfast room in fifteen minutes. I went to the breakfast room and waited for him, but he did not come. I went back to his room and found him there. He was sitting in his favorite chair, with the morning paper upon his lap, but his head had fallen upon his bosom, and his soul had gone out to be with God." Never an ache, never a pain, never needed a doctor—he never took any medicine. Yet in fifteen minutes he had gone out to another world.

Are you ready for that hour to come to you? There is only one way to make preparation: Come to God through Jesus Christ, his only begotten Son, and all will be well with you forever.

2

WHO IS JESUS CHRIST?

And Simon Peter answered and said, Thou art the Christ, the Son of the living God.—MATTHEW 16:16.

Throughout the ages there have been many conjectures and much discussion about the Lord Jesus Christ. Men have asked: "Who is Jesus? Who is this One who claims the attention of all the world? Who is this mighty Man who has such an abiding place in the hearts of countless millions of people?"

There have been many views about Jesus. Some have said that he was mad, that he was insane, that he was in league with Beelzebub, the prince of devils. But others have said that he was exactly what he claimed to be, Jesus Christ, the Son of the living God. One day he called his disciples to him and said to them, "Whom do men say that I the Son of man am?" They answered: "Some say that you are John the Baptist; some say that you are Elijah, and others say that you are Jeremiah." "But whom say ye that I am?" he asked them. And then Peter, the spokesman for the group, said, "Thou art the Christ, the Son of the living God." This answer greatly pleased Jesus, for he said, "Flesh and blood hath not revealed it unto thee, but my Father which is in heaven."

In this message I cannot tell you all about Jesus Christ. I could not, even in many messages, give to you all the truth about the greatest character of the ages. How can a man encompass the character of Jesus Christ in thirty minutes' time? We can discuss but briefly and simply some of the high points as we endeavor to answer the question, Who is Jesus Christ?

I. He Is a Divine Person

In recent years many critics have risen up, even in prominent pulpits, and have declared that Jesus was not divine. They said that he was a mere man, the fairest flower of evolution, a good man, but just a man after all. These critics get their names upon the front page of the paper for a while, but they soon pass into oblivion, while Jesus Christ, the divine Person, stands out stronger than ever.

1. His Divinity Is Shown by His Life

(1) *He was born of a virgin.*—Look upon that beautiful scene. An angel comes to Mary and tells her that God is going to use her to bring his own Son into the world. Jesus did not have a human father. He was miraculously conceived by the Holy Spirit, and there has never been another birth like this. This was simply God's method of breaking the laws of heredity. His birth shows us that God isn't subject to any human or physical limitations.

We marvel at his birth, and we cannot explain it outside the supernatural power of God. In Genesis 18:14 we read these words: "Is any thing too hard for God?" No, there is nothing too hard for God. He had the power to break down every natural law and cause his Son to be born of a virgin.

(2) *He had a sinless character.*—First Peter 2:22: "Who did no sin, neither was guile found in his mouth." Hebrews 4:15: "For we have not an high priest which cannot be touched with the feeling of our infirmities; but was in all points tempted like as we are, yet without sin."

There have been many good men in the world, but none has been perfect like Jesus. Every man that ever lived has sinned. All the saints in glory have sinned, but there was no sin in Jesus. Sin separates from God; but Jesus had unbroken fellowship with the Father because he did no sin. No man could ever say that Jesus spoke, thought, or acted sinfully. We must bow with Pilate before Jesus' matchless life and say, "I find in him no fault at all."

(3) *He performed unheard-of miracles.*—The Bible records thirty-five miracles which Jesus performed. He gave sight to the blind; he gave a new body to the cripple; he gave life to the dead. Nicodemus said one night, "No man can do these miracles . . . , except God be with him." Nicodemus was right—this man is a divine Person. The world has seen many magicians, but none who could perform the miracles which Jesus performed.

(4) *He died a sacrificial death.*—I grant you that many men have made their sacrifices, but none so great as the sacrifice which he made. Life was sweet to Jesus, but the salvation of the world was sweeter.

Love is one of God's great attributes, and he showed forth his love in giving. Jesus died, not because he wanted to, not because he deserved to die, but because he loved us with a divine love. The thief on the cross saw how he died, and said, "Lord, remember me." The captain of the soldiers saw how he died, and said, "Truly this man was the Son of God." You and I look upon his death and say, "Greater love hath no man than this."

(5) *He arose from the dead.*—His resurrection climaxes every claim made for his divinity. No man but Christ has risen from the dead under his own power.

In the old days a Frenchman cried out, "Why will men follow Christ and not me and my teachings?" The answer came back, "If you will die and come back alive from the grave in three days, men will follow you as they do Christ." But no man can do it save Jesus alone. He conquered death and the grave because he was divine.

(6) *He ascended to heaven.*—On Mount Olivet he raised his hands in blessing, a cloud surrounded him, and upon the bosom of that cloud he went back to the Father from whence he came. He did not go down to rest in a grave as other men do, but he climbed the starry heights on wings of power because he was divine. No one was born as he was born. He lived a sinless life. He performed unheard-of miracles. He died a sacrificial death. He rose from the grave and ascended upon high. He must indeed be the divine Son of God.

2. His Divinity Is Shown by His Own Claims

(1) *He claimed to exist with the Father before the foundation of the world.*—In his great prayer in John 17, he spoke of the glory that he had with the Father before the world began. In John 1:1 we go back into the ages before the world was made, and we hear that "in the beginning was the Word, and the Word was with God, and the Word was God." When God said, "Let us make man in our own image," Jesus was present with him as a part of the Trinity.

(2) *He claimed to be God.*—He said, "He that hath seen me hath seen the Father." The age-long cry of humanity has been, "Show us the Father." Christ came revealing the character of God. He came saying: "I am God uncovered; I am God in the flesh; I have come down to earth that man might find and know the Holy One of heaven."

(3) *He claimed to be able to forgive sins.*—No one can do that except God, but Christ as God took this upon himself.

While Christ was preaching one day, a man was let down in his presence from the roof top. Jesus said to

the man, "Thy sins be forgiven thee." Immediately the
Pharisees began to murmur, saying, "No one can forgive
sins but God." For once they were right. But in order
to show that he was God, Christ said, "Son, not only are
thy sins forgiven thee, but now you can rise up and
walk." No one can forgive sin except God, and Jesus
forgave sin; therefore he is God.

(4) *He claimed to merit first place in the lives of men.*
—He gave men to understand that if they followed him,
they must forsake,all and love him above all. He told
them that he should be the first and the foremost in every
walk of life. No mere man can lay claim to all man's
loyalty in this way; but Christ was worthy of all honor
and all praise and all loyalty, for he was the divine Son
of God.

(5) *He claimed to be the Judge of the world.*—This
great function cannot be claimed by anyone other than
God. God has three mighty functions—that of creation,
that of preservation, and that of judgment. These three
functions were all claimed and exercised by Christ.

We must, therefore, admit that Christ is divine, that
he is the greatest miracle of all the ages. We must admit
that his claims are true, or that he is the biggest impostor
in the world. We may question his divinity or doubt
his virgin birth, but the fact still remains that the world
has never seen a man like Jesus, for he is indeed the
divine Son of the divine Father.

A man who has a good pure wife may question the fact
of her goodness and purity. Despite his doubts, her
character isn't changed; she is still good and pure. Men
have doubted Christ, they have said all manner of evil
things against him, but he still remains the divine Son
of God.

II. HE IS GOD COME DOWN TO THE WORLD IN THE FLESH

We read that "the Word was made flesh." Let us look at some of the proofs that Christ is God.

1. The Same Names Were Used of Jesus as Were Used of God.

(1) In Isaiah 44:6, God is speaking, and says: "I am the first, and I am the last." In Revelation 22:13, we hear Jesus say, "I am, . . . , the first and the last."

(2) In the twenty-fourth Psalm we hear this question, "Who is this King of glory?" And the answer comes back, "The Lord of hosts, he is the King of glory." In 1 Corinthians 2:8 we read that "they crucified the Lord of glory." God and Jesus are spoken of in the same terms.

(3) In Romans 9:5 we read that "Christ is over all, God blessed for ever."

2. God Has Five Definite Attributes—Christ Has Them All.

(1) *God is omnipotent.*—We find that omnipotence is also ascribed to Jesus. While he was upon the earth, he had power over disease and death, over the winds and the waves.

(2) *God is omniscient.*—This attribute is ascribed to Jesus. The woman at the well found out that Jesus knew all the secrets of her heart. God is the only One who possesses all knowledge, so we know that Christ is God.

(3) *God is omnipresent.*—He is at all places at the same time. It is even so with Jesus. He tells us that he will be wherever two or three are gathered together in his name. He tells believers that he will be with them

"even unto the end of the age," wherever they may be. He is at all places at all times.

(4) *God is eternal.*—In Genesis 1:1, we read the words, "In the begining [was] God." In John 1:1, "In the beginning was the Word." Moses said, "I Am hath sent me." Jesus said, "Before Abraham was, I Am."

(5) *God is immutable.*—He never changes. But we also read of Jesus that he is "the same yesterday, today, and for ever." Jesus possesses every characteristic of God; therefore he is God.

3. There Are Seven Things Which God Alone Can Do, and Yet Christ Does Them All

He creates, he preserves, he forgives sin, he raises the dead, he transforms bodies, he pronounces judgment, and he bestows eternal life.

4. Christ Received the Same Worship, Faith, and Loyalty Which Were Due to God Alone

He taught that men should worship God only; yet he accepted this worship for himself. In the book of Revelation we see the redeemed hosts of heaven worshiping the Lamb even as they worshiped the Father. We read in Hebrews 1:6; "Let all the angels worship him"; and the writer is speaking of Jesus. Surely One who merits the worship of angels and men is God himself.

III. He Is a Person—A Real Man

This is where Jesus comes right up close to every one of us. Often he may seem far away, but he is a real man and is just as approachable as the dearest friend of our hearts.

1. He Had a Human Parentage

We read in Luke 2:7 that "she [Mary] brought forth her firstborn son." Though he was supernaturally conceived, he was indeed Mary's Son. She was as truly his mother as God was his Father. He had a human parentage as truly as a divine parentage. In order to come close to us and to help us in every time of need, he had to be human, so God gave him a human parentage.

2. He Had a Human Physical Nature

The Bible says that Jesus hungered, he thirsted, he wept, he prayed, he had compassion, he rejoiced, he suffered, he died, and he was buried. We know that he had a physical body and a real, physical human nature.

Because Jesus was human, he knows about our human sufferings and temptations. He was the only perfect and complete human being who ever lived. When you suffer, remember that he suffered and can comfort you. When you are tempted, remember that he was tempted and can help you find a way of escape. Hebrews 2:18 says, "For in that he himself hath suffered being tempted, he is able to succour them that are tempted."

Christ was human so that he could understand us. He was divine so that he could help us. And so in all the troubles and cares of life, let us remember that he is our Elder Brother, our Companion, and our Friend.

IV. HE IS THE SAVIOUR OF MAN

1. He Came into the World for This Purpose

"The Son of man is come to seek and to save that which was lost." "Thou shall call his name Jesus: for he shall save his people from their sins."

I thank God that he is my Saviour. I had sinned—I was on the road to hell, but in his wondrous grace he saved me and made me his child. How do you look upon him? Is he the Saviour of the world, or is he your

Saviour? Is he your own personal Saviour? If not, then, so far as you are concerned, he died in vain.

2. He Is Carrying On This Work Daily

In human hearts the world over he is working through his Spirit to save men. He knows his people, and he is calling them by name. Is he calling you? Is he working in your heart? Don't resist him, for to do so is to die.

V. He Is Our Daily Strength

1. He Gives Us Power to Live

No man can really live without his help. Jesus is the only One who can give us the power to live as we should from day to day. He does give that power, as every child of God can testify.

2. He Satisfies the Deepest Longings of Our Souls

In every heart there is a longing for a better life. The world of money, fame, power, and pleasure cannot satisfy this deep longing. He alone can satisfy our longings and speak peace to our hearts.

3. He Intercedes for Us

"He ever lives to make intercession for us." I came from a very large family. There were many boys but only one girl. It was only natural, therefore, that our sister could get closer to our father than anyone else. He always listened to her. Many a time when I wanted some special permission or favor from my father, I would not approach him directly, but I told my sister about it and she interceded for me. So it is that when we have sinned, Jesus Christ is there closer to God the Father than anyone else, interceding for us at the throne of grace. That is what he is doing right now—making intercession for us.

VI. He Is the Coming King

When he went back into heaven, the men in white said to the disciples: "This same Jesus, . . . shall so come in like manner as ye have seen him go into heaven." All through the New Testament this fact rings out—Jesus is coming again! He is coming in the air to take unto himself forever all those who have believed in his matchless name. Later he is coming in glory with his saints to reign forever and ever. Will you be ashamed at his coming? What will you be doing when Jesus comes back?

VII. He Is the World's Final Judge

At the judgment seat of Christ, he will judge the works of all believers. And at the judgment of the great white throne, he will judge those who have left him out of their lives. Every man must face one of these judgments, either to be rewarded or to be cast out into eternal suffering forever.

Today I come to hand to you a loving invitation—you are invited to come to Christ and to receive the good things he has for his children. If you reject him, in the great day of judgment you will be summoned to appear before him. Are you ready for that great day to come? Are you ready to stand before Jesus Christ who died for you and whom you have rejected? "Be ye also ready: for in such an hour as ye think not the Son of man cometh."

Who is Jesus? He is God himself. He is a wonderful person. He is a gracious Saviour. He is our daily strength—our coming King and our final Judge. But the main question is this: Is he your Saviour today?

A dear old Scotchman lay dying. His eyes were closed; he seemed to be oblivious of everything and every person around him. His wife went to the bedside and whispered in his ear, "Dinna ye ken your wee wifey?" There was no response from the old man. His daughter then whispered these words, "Dinna ye ken your wee daughter?" Still there was no response. His pastor then went to the bedside and, whispering in his ear, he said, "Sandy, dinna ye ken Jesus Christ?" The eyes opened up, a smile played about his face, and the old man said, "Aye, I ken him—he is my ain dear Saviour!"

My friend, can you say that today?

3

THE HOLY SPIRIT AND HIS MISSION ON EARTH

And I will pray the Father, and he shall give you another Comforter, that he may abide with you for ever.—JOHN 14:16.

It must have been sweet to live daily with Jesus as the disciples did. They ran to him with every trouble; they brought him every problem, and in all things he spoke peace to their souls. He had a balm for every worry and a cure for every troubled heart. We could wish that we, too, could have walked with Jesus and been blessed by his presence.

But now he is going to die. In the upper room he looks about him and is deeply grieved because of the sorrow overshadowing his friends. He has told them about his going away, but they do not understand it. The news has gone like a dart into their hearts, and they are saying to themselves: "What will we do when he is gone and there will be no one to lead us, to teach us, to comfort us, and to love us with an exceeding great love?" But he must go—he must die—he must be raised again—he must make the sacrifice that would save them forever and ever. Weep, ye disciples, but your Saviour cannot stay with you; he must go away and leave you for a time without a comforter.

It seems that in this hour Jesus would be the one who needed comfort, for he was the One who was facing death. But in this hour, as in every other hour, he thought of others and not of himself. He saw the sorrow of his disciples, and he comforted them. "I am going away,"

25

he said, "but I will send you a Comforter—I will not leave you comfortless—I will not leave you as sheep without a shepherd. I will send one to comfort and sustain you throughout all the days." And in due course of time he sent that Comforter, whose name is the Holy Spirit.

I come to you to talk about this Promised One, about the Holy Spirit and his mission on earth. This subject ought to interest every Christian; yet there are few Christians who know much about the Holy Spirit. As a child I heard the ministers speak about the Holy Spirit, and I had a very vague idea of what they meant. Some Christians have indulged in such extreme fanaticism concerning this subject as to cause others to shy away from it. But it is precious to know the Holy Spirit as a person and to feel him in your heart. He is my Friend, even as Jesus is my Friend, and I want to introduce him to you today. I want you to meet him, to know who he is and what he does. The best and simplest definition I know for the Holy Spirit is this: The Holy Spirit is God in the human heart.

I. WHO IS THE HOLY SPIRIT?

1. The Holy Spirit Is a Person

We are never to speak of the Spirit as "it" any more than we speak of Jesus or God as "it." He isn't something emanating or flowing from God, but he is a real person.

(1) *The fact that he is a person is shown by the uses of his name.*—When we baptize a person, we baptize him in the name of the "Father and of the Son and the Holy Spirit." We use the name of the Spirit right along with the names of Jesus and of God. When we pronounce a benediction, which we get from the Bible, we again use the name of the Spirit in the same manner in which we use the name of God and of Christ. If the Holy Spirit is merely

an influence, we would not mention him along with these other two great names. God and Christ are persons, and we connect the Spirit's name right along with their names because the Spirit is also a person.

(2) *The fact that he is a person is shown by his appearances on earth.*—I see Jesus go down into the waters of the Jordan. John the Baptist baptizes him beneath these waters. When he comes up out of the water, the doors of heaven open, a bright light shines upon him, a flood of glory descends and rests upon the sacred head of our Saviour. The Spirit came in the form of a dove, symbolizing gentleness and purity. The Spirit was *seen* by the brink of the river, even as Jesus came up out of the water, and as God spoke from heaven.

Some years later we see a company of disciples in the upper room. Jesus has gone on to heaven and these disciples are waiting for the coming of the Spirit as promised by the Saviour. The sound of a rushing mighty wind suddenly fills the house, a bright light shines about them, and cloven tongues as of fire sit upon each of them. This was a marvelous appearance of the Holy Spirit in person. An influence cannot appear, nor can an influence be seen. The Holy Spirit was there in person.

(3) *The fact that he is a person is shown by the personal characteristics ascribed to him.*—Knowledge is ascribed to the Spirit. First Corinthians 2:11: "The things of God knoweth no man, but the Spirit of God." *Will* is ascribed to the Spirit. First Corinthians 12:11: the "Spirit, dividing to every man severally as he will." God has certain spiritual gifts for men. The Spirit wills that they should be given to certain men, and the Spirit does give them to certain men. *Mind* is ascribed to the Spirit. Romans 8:27: "He that searcheth the hearts knoweth what is the mind of the Spirit." *Power* is ascribed to the Spirit. Romans 15:13: "Now the God of hope fill you

with all joy and peace in believing, that ye may abound in hope, through the power of the Holy Ghost." Now we know that the Holy Spirit is a person because he knows, he wills, he has power, and he exercises the functions of a mind.

(4) *The fact that he is a person is shown by the acts and deeds ascribed to him.*—In the first chapter of the Bible we read that "the Spirit of God moved upon the face of the waters" and *brought order* out of chaos. Once there was no order—the earth was like a valley of darkness under the shadow of death. It was then that God, the Holy Spirit, brooded over the earth. He sowed the seeds of life and brought forth every tree, every plant, and every living thing. He *inspired* the writing of the Bible. "Holy men of God spake as they were moved by the Holy Ghost." Moses wrote the Pentatauch, but the Holy Spirit moved his hand. David wrote the Psalms, and Solomon wrote the Proverbs, but they were moved by the Holy Spirit. Isaiah and Jeremiah and others wrote the Old Testament prophecies, but they wrote only as they were inspired by the Spirit. He *guided* God's servants. In Antioch the Holy Spirit said to the church, "Separate me Barnabas and Saul [and send them out upon a missionary journey]." The Holy Spirit spoke to Peter and said, "Go down to the centurion and preach the gospel of the Gentiles." The Holy Spirit spoke to Paul and said, "Don't go back into Asia, but go over into Macedonia."

(5) *The fact that he is a person is shown by the fact that he is treated as a person.*—The Spirit can be *grieved*. Ephesians 4:30: "Grieve not the holy Spirit of God." The Spirit can be *resisted*. Acts 7:51: "Ye do always resist the Holy Spirit." The Holy Spirit can be *lied to*. Peter said to Ananias in Acts 5:3, "Why hath Satan filled thy heart to lie to the Holy Spirit?" All these facts teach us that

the Holy Spirit is a person. He is not an influence, not an attribute, but a real person. We are to think of him, then, as a person, and we are to seek to know him and to give ourselves in full surrender to him.

2. The Holy Spirit Is God, the Third Person of the Trinity

This is something that we will never fully understand —this mystery of God the Father, God the Son, and God the Holy Spirit. We worship him as one God; yet he is in three persons. God the Father is the mind, God the Son is the body, and God the Spirit is the soul.

(1) *The Spirit is shown to be God by the four divine attributes ascribed to him.*—These attributes are omnipotence, omniscience, omnipresence, and eternity. These attributes belong to God, and they are also ascribed to the Holy Spirit, proving to us that the Spirit is God.

(2) *The Holy Spirit is shown to be God by the three divine works which are ascribed to God only.*—Only God can create; yet in Job 33:4 we read, "The Spirit of God hath made me." Only God can impart life, but we read that "God . . . breathed into his nostrils the breath of life; and man became a living soul." This breath is God's Spirit. Only God can be the author of divine prophecies; and yet we are told in 2 Peter 1:21 that no prophecy came by the will of men, but man spoke for God, being moved by the Holy Spirit. Only God can do these things, and yet the Holy Spirit does them. And so the Holy Spirit is God.

(3) *The Holy Spirit is shown to be God by the fact that the same passages in the Old Testament which refer to God, in the New Testament refer to the Holy Spirit.*

(4) *The Holy Spirit is shown to be God by the way in which his name is coupled with that of God and Christ in the formula for baptism and in the Bible benediction.*

—The Spirit's name is coupled in equality with that of the Father and the Son.

Do you see who he is? He is a person just as Jesus is a person. He is God just as the Heavenly Father is God, even though he shows not himself to any man. Jesus is not here in the flesh today, but the Holy Spirit is here taking his place. He is a person, and he is God.

Where is he today? Is he lying idle? No, he is existent everywhere; but, most of all and best of all, he lives in the hearts of believers. He sees a weary soul and whispers, "Come unto Jesus and rest." He sees eyes that are filled with tears, and he wipes away the tears and bids the saddened heart to look to Jesus. He sees a tempest-tossed soul and speaks the word of consolation. He, conjoined with the Father and the Son, is working for the salvation of souls and the edification of the saints. He is a living being, a divine person.

II. WHAT DOES THE HOLY SPIRIT DO IN THE WORLD?

1. He Convicts of Sin

No man can do this, no minister can do it. The minister can come to you with the sharp blade of the truth and thrust it deep into your heart, but he cannot convict you of sin; only the Holy Spirit can do this. A Christian goes to the home of a hardened sinner—a man who has no use for the gospel or the church of God. The Christian talks—he prays with the sinner—he reads the Bible to him—he weeps over him. The sinner is saved, but the Christian did not do it—the conviction came because of the power of the Holy Spirit. We are to do the best we can in soul-winning, but only the Holy Spirit can bring conviction for sin. John 16:8: "And when he is come, he will reprove the world of sin, and of righteousness, and of judgment." When you feel that you have sinned and that you want to be a Christian—when the weight of your guilt bears down upon you, the Holy Spirit is then convicting you and you should not resist him.

2. He Calls Us to Eternal Life

Revelation 22:17: "The Spirit and the bride say, Come." He calls men out of their sin; he calls them to eternal life. He is calling in many ways even now. It is he who puts the desire for heaven and for eternal life in the human heart.

3. He Regenerates

To be saved, a man must be born of the Spirit. The Holy Spirit alone can give you a new birth. God makes men, the devil unmakes him, and the Spirit remakes him. God creates, the devil destroys, and the Spirit recreates. He takes away the old life and gives the new life.

4. He Seals Us unto the Day of Redemption

Ephesians 4:30: "Grieve not the holy Spirit of God, whereby ye are sealed unto the day of redemption." A man makes out his will, a seal is put upon it. When he dies, the will is opened up. When we come to Christ, the Holy Spirit seals us; and no man on earth can break that seal, for when he seals us unto the day of redemption, he causes us to become the children of God forever.

5. He Causes Us to Remember

John 14:26 "But the Comforter, which is the Holy Ghost, whom the Father will send in my name, he shall teach you all things, and bring all things to your remembrance, whatsoever I have said unto you." Memory is a wonderful thing. We often return to a higher and better life because of the magical workings of memory. Jesus wanted us to remember. He wanted us to remember the things he said and did while he was here, and so he sent the Holy Spirit to cause us to remember. When we come to celebrate the Lord's Supper, the Holy Spirit broods over this memorial meal, causing us to remember that Jesus died and that he is coming again. We are prone to forget all that Christ has done for us, but the Spirit often reminds us of his sacrifice, thus causing us to love him more and more.

6. He Teaches Us God's Will

Jesus said, "He will teach you all things." The real Christian wants to know the will of God. The Spirit in his heart teaches him this will. Jesus Christ was the greatest teacher that the world has ever known, but when he went away, he said, "I am going to send you another Teacher—One who is infallible—One who will lead you into all truth."

If you want to know to what church you should belong, let the Spirit teach you. If you want to know how to be baptized, let the Spirit teach you. If you want to know how much money to give to Christ's kingdom, let the Spirit teach you. If you are in doubt about anything, let the Spirit teach you. The Holy Spirit never makes a mistake, and he will teach you God's will if you will give him the chance.

7. He Comforts in Time of Sorrow

Jesus said, "I will send you a comforter." In the hours of our sorrow our friends and loved ones do their best to comfort us, but, after all, the Holy Spirit is the great Comforter. When we sit in the shadows, he is the only One who can give comfort to our broken hearts.

Sometime ago I was riding on a train through the mountains. The sun was shining brightly and the light was streaming into every window. In a few minutes the porter came in and turned the lights on in the car. I wondered why he was turning on these lights when there was so much light on the outside. It didn't take me long to learn the reason—in a few minutes the train plunged into the darkness of a tunnel. If we had not had the lights on the inside, we would have been in total darkness.

The noonday light of the world may be shining brightly in your life right now, but what will you do when you are plunged into the hour of sorrow and darkness? You need a light on the inside—you need the Holy Spirit. They tell us time is a great healer, but the Holy Spirit is a surer and greater Comforter.

Some years ago a friend of mine, a splendid Christian man, lay dying. He called his wife and children to the bedside, told each of them good-by, gave them some kindly advice, and then offered a prayer with them before he died. As they went down into their Gethsemane of sorrow, there was no murmur nor bitterness—they felt the Holy Spirit by their side comforting their hearts. There are others who, when they have a deep sorrow, can find no comfort. They do not know which way to turn because they do not know the great comfort of the Holy Spirit. Oh, sorrowing one, yield your heart to him—he will give you comfort!

8. He Gives Us Power to Overcome the Devil

I have heard many men say, "I haven't power to live the Christian life." No man can in himself ever find that power; it must come from above. When we go to Christ and ask for help, he guarantees a power which is greater than the power of Satan.

9. He Empowers Us for Service

A man stands to preach the blessed gospel. The power of God is upon him, and souls are blessed and saved.

Where did he get that spiritual power? Did he receive it along with his college degree? No. Did he receive it from his books or seminary training? No, that power came from above. The Holy Spirit is the One who empowers us for service. Let a man try to preach in his own power, and he simply beats the air. Every true preacher knows what I am talking about. We must serve in his power, or we have no power at all. We cannot win men with our own words or our own wisdom —we need the power of the Holy Spirit. If you feel weak as you attempt his service, just remember that he has promised that the Holy Spirit will be your power.

Here in the church we have a number of brilliant electric lights. There is absolutely no power in the electric bulbs, nor in the wiring, nor in the filaments; yet I can push the switch on the wall and the church is flooded with light. This means that back yonder behind the electric fixtures and the wire there is a great power which furnishes this illumination. There is no power in you and me apart from the Holy Spirit. There is no spiritual power in our brains and bodies and hearts, but in Christ there is great power, and if we surrender these instruments to him, he can flood the world with a great spiritual light.

Christians, the Holy Spirit is a person. Do you really and truly know him? Does he have an influence in your life? You may know him through prayer and through the surrender of yourself to him. Luke 11:13: "If ye then, being evil, know how to give good gifts unto your children: how much more shall your heavenly Father give the Holy Spirit to them that ask him?"

The Holy Spirit is not a power for you to use but a power to use you. The question is not, How much of him do you have? How much of you does he have? If you will make a full surrender to him, out of you will flow spiritual power and blessings for the world. To the sinner I would say, Don't trifle with the Holy Spirit. Blasphemy against the Father and Son may be forgiven, but blasphemy against the Holy Spirit can never be forgiven. I don't know what all this means, and the great theologians do not know, but I do know this: If the Holy Spirit calls you, you are not to go on in your sin—you are not to reject his call. If you heed not his call, you are treading on dangerous ground. If the Holy Spirit convicts you of sin, I urge you to listen to him and to turn to the Lamb of God which taketh away the sin of world.

Come now and meet my Friend, the Holy Spirit! Put everything else aside—throw all sin out of your life—cast out all that would grieve him, and you will feel his sweet presence living in your heart. The greatest need of the church today is to have the Holy Spirit sweeping through its members. So let us go to the throne of grace, surrender our lives to him—leave our sins—and thus shall we meet and know and walk with the Friend of friends.

4

HIS SATANIC MAJESTY, THE DEVIL

Ye are of your father, the devil, and the lusts of your
father ye will do. He was a murderer from the beginning,
and abode not in the truth, because there is no truth in
him.—John 8:44.

He that committeth sin is of the devil; for the devil sinneth
from the beginning. For this purpose the Son of God was
manifested, that he might destroy the works of the devil.—
1 John 3:8.

The Bible tells us very little about the origin of the
devil. It seems to infer that he was once an archangel, an
archangel of great power and glory. Because of this high
position, and led on by his arrogance, he became so proud
that God had to cast him out of heaven. Now he is per-
mitted to go about in the world tempting people and
acting as a mighty adversary. This idea is generally accepted by Bible scholars. God created all things good,
but some of his creations became bad—man, for instance.
It is reasonable to believe that the devil was created in
goodness, but that he became evil and was then cast out
of heaven.

He is called by different names—Satan, Beelzebub, the
evil one, the serpent, the dragon—the god of this world
and the prince of this world. It doesn't matter what you
call him—he is the devil just the same.

I. There Is a Devil

Some people say that the devil doesn't exist, that he
is merely a figment of the imagination. The Christian

Scientists tell us that "all is good." However, any sensible person knows that all things are not good, and that there is a mighty being behind all evil, namely, the devil.

1. The Bible Proves His Existence

Jesus said in John 8:44, "The devil is." In Matthew 13:19, where Jesus was explaining the parable of the sower, he said, "The wicked one . . . , catcheth away that which was sown in his heart."

If we say that there is no devil, we make Jesus a liar. Peter said that there is a devil—John and Paul told us of his existence. But Jesus' words are enough for us. To deny the existence of the devil is to deny the truthfulness and trustworthiness of Christ. We know that the devil made his appearance upon the earth. We see him appearing to Job. He appeared to Jesus in the great temptation and at other times. He is shown in the book of Revelation as appearing many times upon the earth.

2. Experience Attests That There Is a Devil

We know from human experience that Satan is on the job, and there is an impulse and a desire in every one of us to follow evil. Does this impulse come from God? No, it comes from the devil. It comes from a source outside God, no matter what name we give to that source.

Every Christian in the world has a continual fight against the forces of evil. He is tempted on every side. These temptations come sometimes even when the child of God is in the holy place of prayer. It is the devil who brings this evil into our minds. Every one of us is confronted every day with the influence and power of a personal devil.

II. The Nature of the Devil

1. He Is a Person

First John 3:8 says, "The devil sinneth." Only a person can be said to sin. This doesn't necessarily mean that he has a body like ours, but he is a person just the same. He knows, he feels, he wills. The cartoonists usually picture the devil as being a red figure with a long tail and a pitchfork. He doesn't appear in that form. If he came in that form, we would know him and avoid him. But when he comes to tempt us, he often comes in beauty and appeals to us in the most attractive way.

We need an armor against the devil. We find this armor in Ephesians 6:11-12, which reads as follows: "Put on the whole armour of God, that ye may be able to stand against the wiles of the devil. For we wrestle not against flesh and blood, but against principalities, against powers, against the rulers of the darkness of this world, against spiritual wickedness in high places."

We are fighting against a real person. Jesus and the whole Bible teach us that he is a person. A system of doctrine without a personal devil is a system which is radically unchristian and unscriptural.

2. He Is a Being of Great Power and Authority

Satan is a strong personality, and we cannot fight him alone. We need all the help of heaven in our combat against the devil. America had a great conflict against Germany and Japan, but World War II was nothing compared to the age-long conflict between the souls of men and this mighty personal being whom we know as Satan. Think of all the crime, the murders, the sorrows, the troubles in the world. What does it all mean? It is simply a part of the great conflict between good and evil.

We must not underestimate the devil. We cannot laugh him off. The big fight is on in our hearts and in the world. Satan is lining up against God and his children and everything good that exists. On the other hand, we must not overestimate the devil. We cannot afford to get blue and pessimistic and say, "The world is going to the devil." We are in a great battle, but He who is for us is greater than the one who fights against us. The devil is mighty, but the Saviour is Almighty. We can overcome through him. The devil does many wicked things, but God will overcome him in the end.

3. He Is a Being of Great Majesty and Dignity of Position

Jude 9 says: "Yet Michael the archangel, when contending with the devil he disputed about the body of Moses, durst not bring against him a railing accusation, but said, The Lord rebuke thee."

It seems that Michael, the archangel of heaven, quarreled with the devil over the body of Moses. We see that the position of Satan was so exalted that even Michael did not dare bring a railing accusation against him, but rather called upon the Lord to rebuke Satan. If an angel who occupied such a high position dared not rebuke Satan, surely Satan's position must have been a high one indeed. Yes, the devil is a person of great majesty and dignity of position.

4. He Is the Prince of This World

This is where we come in contact with him. If he were simply some great monarch ruling a kingdom thousands of miles away from us, we should never need to be concerned about him; but he is right here in this world carrying on his evil work, and we come in contact with him every day. John 14:30: "Hereafter I will not talk much with you: for the prince of this world cometh, and hath nothing in me."

Just look around you for one minute and you will see that the devil is ruling today as the prince of this world. We can never have permanent peace in the world, because he rules in the hearts of the world's great leaders. The worldly man is out for gain; he has a greedy heart and seeks to gain everything available. He has no respect for the rights of others. This is true of individuals and nations, because the devil is ruling in human hearts. Why were nations overrun and millions of people killed in Europe and the Far East during World War II? And why do similar conditions of war and hatred and greed prevail in many parts of the world today? There is only one answer to all these questions: The devil is ruling in the hearts of men all over the world.

The devil has the upper hand in many lives. He sits upon the throne of many hearts. A little girl in Chicago is kidnaped and her body is hacked to pieces—a drunken father kills a little child—a man and woman kill an aged relative in order to get her insurance—a young woman takes the downward trail which leads to ruin and disgrace —an otherwise loving father brings his little family to poverty and distress because of sin. The devil is behind every one of these things. He even comes to church and enters into the hearts of the church members, causing them to do things which only the devil could think of. What a pitiful and tragic thing it is to let the devil rule in the heart in place of the Lord Jesus Christ!

III. THE CHARACTER OF THE DEVIL

1. He Is Wicked

God is the Holy One; he is the embodiment of perfect holiness. The devil is just the opposite; he is the embodiment of consummate wickedness.

2. He Is the Original Sinner

First John 3:8 says: "He that committeth sin is of the devil; for the devil sinneth from the beginning. For this purpose the Son of God was manifested, that he might destroy the works of the devil."

Why do men sin today? It is because they belong to the devil; they have his nature in their flesh. Why, then, do Christians sin? They have been saved, but they still retain their old sinful natures. They never lose that nature until Jesus in the twinkling of an eye transforms them and makes them like unto himself. The evil nature within the Christian is always fighting against the good nature—the spiritual nature. The flesh of this world sins—the divine spirit within a Christian repents. When I sin, my flesh has the upper hand. When I repent of that sin, my spirit is ruling. The devil tempts the Christian, and the Christian often falls into sin. He can say, however, with Paul, "It is no more I that do it, but the sin that dwelleth in me." The Christian who sins is indeed a wretched man, but he can say again with Paul, "I thank God that through Jesus Christ our Lord I can be delivered from the body of this death."

IV. THE WORK OF THE DEVIL

1. He Lies to Men

We are told that he is the "father of lies." We cannot trust anyone who tells lies, for the devil has invented every lie that has ever been told. He lies to men today. He says to them, "Follow me into the pathways of sin and I will give you the sweetness of life." The devil is lying, because he cannot do it. He can give you the pleasures of sin for a season, but in the end you drink the bitter dregs of disappointment and despair as you sink down into eternal hell.

Yonder is an old man, bent and gray. Once he was young with all of life lying out before him. But the devil lied to him. The devil told him about the good things he could have if he would follow the ways of sin and the world. The young man said, "I will take it all in." He drank from every flower of sin—he tasted the sweetness of every fountain of iniquity—he wasted his years in riotous living. Now he has nothing left but the bitter memories of a misspent life. He has no joy in the present, he has no hope for the future. It has been well said that the devil has no happy old people.

2. He Tempts Men to Sin

He is the original tempter. He tempted our first parents in the garden of Eden. They fell before the tempter, and as they sank down into sin, they reached up and took the hand of everybody who would ever be born into the world and pulled them down into sin along with them.

The greatest picture of temptation is shown in the tempting of Jesus. For forty days and nights he had prayed and fasted. He came back into the world weak and hungry. The devil met him and tempted him in the realm of material things when he said, "If thou be the Son of God, command that these stones be made bread." But Jesus beat him back with the words from Deuteronomy. The next time the devil tempted him in the realm of his pride. Taking Jesus to the pinnacle of the Temple, he said to him, "If thou be the Son of God, cast thyself down." Jesus again beat him back with another scriptural answer from the psalms. The next time he tempted Jesus in the realm of desire for power. He took him into a high mountain and said to him, "I will give you all the kingdoms of the world and the glory of them if you will fall down and worship me." Jesus again beat him back with a quotation from the same Old Testament record. In like manner Satan tempts us in all these points. Never a day goes by but that he tempts us to sin in word and thought and deed.

What a shrewd tempter Satan is! He arranges things in a beautiful manner; he captivates and fascinates us. He tries to make us forget that we are Christians; he seeks to make us throw aside our good resolutions; he plants a little thought in our minds—a thought which grows into a deadly sin. The only way we can overcome the tempter is through the power that comes from the Lord Jesus Christ.

3. He Is the Author of False Views

Second Corinthians 4:4 says: "In whom the god of this world hath blinded the minds of them which believe not, lest the light of the glorious gospel of Christ, who is the image of God, should shine unto them."

All over the world the devil has been able to cause men to doubt the old things which have been believed down through the ages. He especially brings doubts concerning the person of Christ; he is constantly telling men that Christ isn't divine. He begins an evil work by planting a doubt in our hearts; then he is easily able to lead us on and on into sin. In the garden of Eden, when the devil tempted Eve, she said to him, "God has told us not to eat of the fruit of this certain tree, saying that if we do eat of it we will die." Then the devil replied in a very sarcastic vein, "Ye shall not surely die." The seed was planted—the doubt began to grow, and soon Eve had been swept down into the guilt of sin. He even tried to bring doubt into Jesus' mind when he said, "*If* thou be the Son of God."

The gambling hells, the liquor joints, the houses of infamy are not the only places of Satan's activities. He is working in many schools and colleges in the land. Men and women are teaching immature boys and girls to doubt the Word of God. They call the Bible "old fogy stuff" and encourage the students to throw off mother's religion. The devil knows that if he can cause these young people to doubt the Bible, he can soon lead them off into sin. I know it is true, for I have seen it many times.

When Dr. B. H. Carroll, founder and first president of the Southwestern Baptist Theological Seminary, lay upon his death bed, he said to Dr. Lee R. Scarborough, his successor, "Lee, keep the Seminary tied to the old Book." We must not let the devil capture our schools. Christ and the Word of God must be the center of our educational life if Christianity is to thrive and if Christian leaders are to be sent into this wicked world.

V. The Destiny of the Devil

Revelation 20:10 says: "And the devil that deceived them was cast into the lake of fire and brimstone, where the beast and the false prophet are, and shall be tormented day and night for ever and ever."

When the devil comes down to his final end, his destiny will be in the everlasting fires of hell. He will not be alone—his followers will be with him. Hell is a "place prepared for the devil and his angels." It is a place of just and righteous punishment. If you go to hell, it will be because you cast your lot with the devil rather than with God. Everyone who rejects Christ is throwing in his lot with Satan, and there is nothing left for him but everlasting hell.

VI. How to Get Victory over the Devil

1. Surrender to God and Resist the Devil

James 4:7: "Submit yourselves therefore to God. Resist the devil, and he will flee from you." When we resist the devil in our own strength, we will always fail. But when we surrender to God, we have all his power on our side. The trouble with most of us is that we do not resist the overtures of Satan. When he tempts us, we embrace the opportunity to sin; but if we are to conquer Satan, we must resist him in the strength of the Lord. We must say to him, "I cannot yield to this thing because I am a child of God." Surely the Lord will help us if we assume such an attitude, and if in that way we whip the devil, we will be a little bit stronger to defeat him the next time.

2. We Are to Store Up God's Word and God's Promises in Our Hearts

Jesus defeated the devil by remembering and resting on the Word of God. We are to remember all the promises which he makes to those who stand up for him. When we neglect the Bible, we are leaving the windows wide open, and the devil can come in and conquer us. God imparts strength through his Word, and we must stand upon that Word if we are to be strong enough to defeat the evil one.

3. We Are to Put On the Whole Armor of God

We can hold the shield of faith before us by saying in our hearts, "This is the victory that overcometh the world, even our faith." We are to wear the helmet of salvation, shouting, "I am saved, I belong to Jesus, and I will not yield to this temptation." We must wield the sword of the Spirit, using the Bible and its truth upon the devil and thus sending him back to his hot hole in hell.

4. We Are to Claim Jesus' Strength for Ours

Ephesians 6:10: "Finally, my brethren, be strong in the Lord, and in the power of his might." When temptations come and we cry out, "Lord, help me," he will give us strength. He has never refused yet to help those who call upon him as they engage in their battles against the prince of this world.

A good Christian man lay dying. Calling his children to the bedside, he had a good word for each of them and then kissed them good-by. Finally he turned to his wife and said to her, "When I am gone, you will trust the Lord and find your comfort in him, won't you?" And she answered, "Yes, dear. 'I know whom I have believed, and am persuaded that he is able to keep that which I have committed unto him against that day!'" Her husband then said: "You and I have been to the cemetery four times to put away those whom we loved, and you will remember that each time as we rode back home God spoke his comfort and grace to us in every turn of the wheels. Now, when I am gone, I know that you will turn to him for your comfort in the hour of sorrow." The good man then began to quote the twenty-third Psalm, and when he came to the verse which says, "Though I walk through the valley of the shadow of death, I will fear no evil," he turned to his wife and said, "Mary, he is with me now and I am going home with him."

He had lived the overcoming life, and now he had gone out to meet his Saviour and to receive his reward.

The devil may be ruling your heart because you do those things which you ought not to do. He may be robbing you of peace and power and comfort. Oh, come to Jesus daily, cast all your cares upon him, put your hand in the nail-pierced hand, and you, too, will be able to live the victorious life.

5

SIN, EARTH'S GREATEST BLOT

Whosoever committeth sin transgresseth also the law: for sin is the transgression of the law.—1 JOHN 3:4.

There is something terribly wrong with this old world in which we are living. We hear about it on every radio news broadcast, we read about it in every newspaper, and friends tell us dark stories of black deeds which they have witnessed. We look all around us and see wickedness rampant on every side. Certainly there is something wrong with the world. We need to realize that this trouble is not on the surface, but that it is deep-seated and internal.

Here is a man in the hospital whose face is pale and drawn. He clutches at the covers and writhes in pain. We say to the doctor: "What is wrong with this man?—he certainly must have some terrible disease. There seems to be nothing wrong with his skin, so the disease must go deeper than that." The doctor then pulls back the cover and shows us the cancer which is eating this man's life away. Then we understand why the face is pale and drawn and why the man clutches at the covers and writhes in pain.

Today we take a look at human society in all its outward manifestations. We see murder, war, deceit, and lust on every side. We look into our own hearts, and we see the same things in a lesser degree. Our conscience tells us that we are not what we ought to be—there is something wrong with every one of us. We are suffering from a dread malady. What is it? The Bible tells us that it is the deep-seated disease called SIN. Even the word has in it the hiss of the serpent. Sin is the greatest blot on the face of the earth.

I. What Is Sin?

1. Sin Is the Transgression of God's Law

This truth is given in our text. Transgress means "to go across." You see a traffic light on the street. The light is shining red, and yet you go across the street just the same. You have transgressed the law—you have broken the law. God's law is our standard. God shows man what is right and what is wrong. The law is straight, but when we go across it, we have sinned—we have transgressed God's law.

Man's laws are fashioned after God's great laws. The law says that we should be honest, that we should not steal. When we are dishonest, we go across the law. God has also said that we should not steal. A man who steals is a criminal before man and God. So it is with all other sins. God has given us the Bible; he has given us a conscience, and he has put it into our hearts to know the difference between right and wrong. The transgression of God's law is sin.

2. Sin Is Rebellion Against God

The prodigal cried out, "I have sinned against heaven, and before thee." David said, "Against thee, thee only, have I sinned." When we sin, we hurt others. When the father sins, he hurts the son. When the son sins, he hurts the father. But our sin is not only against man, but it is also against God; it is rebellion against him. Every sin is a blow upon the heart of God.

Take the matter of worldly indulgences. Unless we can be positive that they are right and acceptable in God's sight, we should not engage in them. What, then, can we do? First Corinthians 10:31: "Whether therefore ye eat, or drink, or whatsoever ye do, do all to the glory of God." We can have a good time in the right way, but we should do nothing of which God would disapprove.

3. Sin Is the Omission of Good

James 4:17: "Therefore to him that knoweth to do good, and doeth it not, to him it is sin." Here is an aged mother who has an only son. That son neglects his mother—he sins away his money. The mother dies; and this son has killed her just as surely as if he had shot her. There are some people who know that they should confess Christ as Saviour, that they should follow him in baptism, that they should be active church members, that they should tithe. However, they refuse to do any of these things. This means they have sinned against the Lord who loved them.

When a little child is sick and her mother goes about her usual social duties, neglecting the child, if the child should die, we can truly say that she killed it by her neglect. You can kill a soul through neglect also. On a little card I saw the question, "What must I do to be lost?" And the answer was, "Nothing." You know that you should repent of your sins and trust Christ as your Saviour, but if you do nothing about it, you will be eternally lost. Sin, therefore, is omission of good.

4. Unbelief Is Sin

The greatest sin in the world isn't murder—men have been forgiven for that sin. However, if you go to your grave an unbeliever, there is no hope for you. Unbelief leads all other sins and is the cause of all other sins. Unbelief is the sin which damns souls.

A father gives many good things to his ungrateful son. The son isn't satisfied, and the father gladly gives him all that he has. In spite of all this goodness, the son comes in and brutally slaps the face of his father. We would call him a base ingrate and say that he is a sinner of the worst type. The Lord blesses us and gives us many good things, and then, as a climax, he gives us his best gift, the Lord Jesus Christ. If we will not accept him and follow him, we are slapping God's face and breaking God's heart. Yes, sin is the greatest blot on the face of the earth—it hurts and damns and dooms forever.

II. Who Commits Sin?

Let four brief passages of Scripture tell us. Romans 3:23: "All have sinned, and come short of the glory of God." Ecclesiastes 7:20: "There is not a just man upon earth, that doeth good, and sinneth not." Isaiah 53:6: "All we like sheep have gone astray." Galatians 3:22: "But the scripture hath concluded all under sin."

The greatest and the best men in the Bible sinned. Moses sinned, David sinned, Paul sinned. There was only One who never sinned—Jesus Christ, God's only Son.

Yonder on the fairgrounds you see a merry-go-round. A rich man is riding a horse, a poor girl is riding a camel, and a little child is riding in a chariot. All are going around in the same direction, and all are controlled by the same central electric power. So it is in real life—the sinful millionaire and the sinful poor girl and the sinful little child are all going in the same direction, and they are controlled by the same central power. The name of that power is SIN.

You cannot show me a man who doesn't commit sin. The sin of the unsaved man may be an outward sin, and the sin of the saved man may be an inward sin. Their sin may differ in degree, but they are both sinners under

the skin. A real Christian does sin, and the more consecrated he is, the more quickly he feels sin. Would you
like to argue on this point? Then let us ask Paul, the
greatest Christian this world has ever known. He says,
"The good that I would I do not: but the evil which I
would not, that I do." What is the answer? Here it is.
Paul speaks again, and he says: "It is no more I that do it,
but sin that dwelleth in me." He said that God had
given him a spiritual nature, but that he saw another
law in his body, even the law of sin. Then he says,
"I myself serve the law of God; but with the flesh the law
of sin."

Before a man is saved, he has only one nature—the
nature of sin. If he is saved, he has two natures within
him. These two natures are constantly warring the one
against the other. The sinful nature often overcomes the
spiritual nature; but, thanks be unto God, the spiritual
nature will win out in the end. In that day when we
see Jesus face to face, the old sinful nature will be laid
aside forever and we shall be like unto him. Now, let
us get this straight. The new nature does not sin—"That
which is born of God commits no sin." The soul has
been born again and it doesn't sin; the body hasn't been
born again, and the body does commit sin. The old
sinful nature is still there, and can be overcome only
through the power of Christ.

III. From Where Does Sin Come?

1. Sin Comes from the Devil

It was he who brought sin and ruin into the garden of
Eden. Once man was made in the sinless image of God,
but now he is in the likeness of Adam, his sinful parent.
"In Adam all die."

2. Sin Comes from the Sinful Nature of Man

Matthew 15:18: "But those things which proceed out of the mouth come forth from the heart; and they defile the man." Sin comes from a sinful heart. If the heart is wrong, the whole life is wrong. Dr. John A. Broadus tells about being in the city of Jerusalem one day when he heard the cry of a little babe. He saw this child lying in the grass and went over to pick him up and to soothe his fears. As he reached down to lift up the little child, he heard the startling cry, "Unclean! Unclean!" He knew what that cry meant, and he did not pick up the little child. The baby was the child of leprous parents and although he seemed to be a healthy and ruddy-cheeked child, the germ of leprosy was deep within his nature and would some day come out to eat his vital life away. So it is that deep down in the nature of everyone of us there is this thing called sin. Sooner or later it will crop out in everyone of us. Yes, sin arises from a sinful nature.

IV. What Is the Penalty of Sin?

1. Physical Death Is the First Penalty of Sin

God said to Adam, "If you eat of this tree, you will surely die." In the course of time he ate of the forbidden fruit, and in due time he died. If he had not sinned, there would have been no death in the world. And while Adam may not have been here now, he would never have tasted death, but might have been translated even as Enoch or Elijah. If this original sin had not come into the world, you and I today would not be forced to go through the suffering which brings death.

2. The Penalty of Sin Is Spiritual Death and Eternal Suffering

"The wages of sin is death." "The soul that sinneth, it shall die." When man sins his life away, there is nothing left for him but to perish forever in eternal hell.

Psalm 9:17: "The wicked shall be turned into hell, and all the nations that forget God."

Daniel 12:2: "And many of them that sleep in the dust of the earth shall awake, some to everlasting life, some to shame and everlasting contempt."

Revelation 20:15: "And whosoever was not found written in the book of life was cast into the lake of fire."

Revelation 21:8: "But the fearful, and unbelieving, and the abominable, and murderers, and whoremongers, and sorcerers, and idolaters, and all liars, shall have their part in the lake which burneth with fire and brimstone."

Revelation 20:10: "And [they] shall be tormented day and night for ever and ever."

The truth of these passages is enough to make any man tremble and flee to Christ for mercy. The man who sins on and on, who rejects Christ continually and finally, will certainly be carried to hell with the murderers and all other sinners.

Before we pass from this subject, let me say that the sin of a Christian will find him out right here. "Be sure your sin will find you out." We pay dearly for every second of sin. "The sin ye do two by two ye pay for one by one." "The mills of the gods grind slowly, but they grind exceeding small."

V. WHAT IS THE REMEDY FOR SIN?

1. Education Is Not the Remedy for Sin

There are those today who say: "Sin comes because of ignorance. Let us educate people, and they will not sink down into sin." However, some of the biggest crooks in the country have been the best educated men. Education of the head doesn't make a change of the heart. A certain man had a rabbit dog which he trained to hunt birds. One day he went with this dog out into the fields hunting quail. The dog happened to run across a rabbit's trail and ran off after the rabbit just as fast as he could go. He had been trained to hunt birds, but when the temptation came, the old nature asserted itself. You can train a man and teach him how he ought to live, but if his heart hasn't been changed, his old nature will assert itself and he will fall before temptation.

2. Good Environment Is Not the Remedy for Sin

We often say, "Let's take this man away from his old companions and old environment and take him away to a new place, and certainly he will live a good life." This doesn't work either, because sin and self are still there. You can give a pig a good bath, tie a ribbon around his neck and put him in your best room, but if you give him the chance he will go back to his mudhole. This is his nature. You can change a man's environment, but unless man's heart is changed, he will go back every time to his old sin. Environment is not the remedy for sin.

3. Jesus Christ Is the Real Remedy for Sin

"Ye must be born again." Get the heart right and the life will come right. Preachers do not need to preach on every little sin in the world—we do need to preach Christ. If men get right with him, all these other matters will straighten out.

(1) *He saves from the guilt of sin.*—"There is therefore now no condemnation to them which are in Christ Jesus." He paid the price in his blood and frees us from our guilt. He justifies us by faith and makes us as if we had never sinned. He forgives and forgets our sins.

No longer does he hold us guilty, but the dark page of our sin is covered by the crimson blood that flowed from Calvary's cross.

(2) *He saves us from the power of sin.*—It is only through Christ that we can find the victory that overcomes sin. When we come against the tempter, we have no strength of our own—we need his help. Sometime ago I saw a picture of a great wheel which was turning round and round. This wheel was filled with gamblers, drunkards, and other sinners. In the center was the devil turning the wheel around. On the outside of the wheel the preachers and other Christian workers were trying to stop the wheel. Underneath the picture was this sign: "Its human nature—you can't stop it." Yes, its human nature, but human nature distorted by sin and ruled by the devil. But the devil can be defeated, and the nature can be made right when Jesus comes in.

(3) *He saves from the penalty of sin.*—The old preacher was right when he said: "I don't know much theology, but I do know that if you go on in your sin without Christ, you will miss heaven and hit hell." There is no hell for us if we are trusting Christ. It is closed forever to the believer. Though we are guilty, though we deserve hell, we are delivered from its penalty because of the One who died on the cross for us.

God could have used some other means of revealing himself to the world, but he chose his only begotten Son to come and die for us. We ask him the question: "How will you go into the world? Will you go as an angel of light and woo men away from their sins?" And he answers: "No, I will go in the form of a servant. I will go in the garment of human flesh. I will make myself one with the sinful creatures of earth; and though I am without sin, I will be obedient unto death, even the death of the cross." He comes down to the world. He lives his life. He comes to the end of the way. Now I see him bowing his back before the smiter. I see him endure the mockery, the blows, the crown of thorns. I see him placed upon the cross and I hear him cry out, "My God, my God, why hast thou forsaken me?" I know then that he is making an offering for sin and that he is tasting death in order that we might be forever free.

I look at those three crosses on that lonely hill. On one cross is a sinner, rejecting Christ, going down to hell. On the central cross is my Saviour, dying in my stead. On the third cross is a thief crying out, "Lord, remember me when thou comest into thy kingdom." One man died in sin, one Man died for sin, and one man was saved from sin. Jesus turned to that poor thief and said, "I will not only remember you, but I will remember and save all those who call on me in faith."

Oh, the wondrous mercy and grace which we find there upon Calvary! Will you call upon Christ? Will you accept him as your Saviour? If not, you are going to hell with this other thief. Oh, trembling, hesitating, sinful soul, come to Christ, and victory over sin will be yours for time and for eternity.

6

THE MYSTERY OF THE NEW BIRTH

Jesus answered and said unto him, Verily, verily I say unto
thee, Except a man be born again, he cannot see the kingdom
of God.—JOHN 3:3.

In the city of Jerusalem there lived a very prominent
man by the name of Nicodemus. He held a high position
in the ranks of the Pharisees. He was a good moral man,
highly respected by everyone. However, in spite of the
honor which had been heaped upon him, his heart was
hungry for something better than the things of this world.
And then there came to this city one day a greater Man—
Jesus of Nazareth, God's only begotten Son. Nicodemus
heard about him and about the new religion which he
taught. He was curious and interested and wanted to
know more about this new faith. So, one night, under the
cover of darkness, he slipped around to the place where
Jesus was staying in order that he might have an in-
terview with him. It never would have done for the
people to see this great man of the Pharisees conversing
with this peasant from Galilee.

Nicodemus was a politician, so he began the conversation with a compliment to Jesus. "We know that you
come from God," he said, "for no man can perform these
miracles that you do except God be with him." Jesus
swept aside the compliment and, looking deep down into
the heart of the hungry-souled man, he said, "Except a
man be born again, he cannot see the kingdom of God."
This puzzled the smart man. He probably expected
Jesus to feel highly honored that he had come to see him.
And now this Teacher had said unto him, "Ye must be

born again." "How can this be?" asked Nicodemus. "Can a man be born when he is old?" And Jesus replied, "That which is born of the flesh is flesh; and that which is born of the Spirit is spirit. [I am speaking to you of a spiritual birth]." And Jesus went on to tell him that if he wanted to be saved and if he wanted to reach heaven, he must believe on the Son of God who was to be lifted up on a cross. In other words, he must be born again. The great man went away secretly believing in Christ in his heart, for we see him coming later to the tomb and assisting in the burial of Christ.

Today many others are like Nicodemus—they have the things of this world, but they are hungering for something better. The same great truth applies to them—they must be born again. Unless they are born again, they cannot be saved; they cannot see heaven. He that is born only once will die twice, but the man who is born twice, born of the flesh and then born of the Spirit, can die but once. The second death has no power over him.

I. What Is the New Birth?

1. The New Birth Is Not Reformation

There are some who say: "You should turn over a new leaf. You should quit your evil life and join the church." My friends, this isn't enough. Many a man reforms; he turns over a new leaf, he leaves the old life of sin, but this is often done for a selfish purpose and is not regeneration. Suppose I owed a certain store $100 and I told them that I would continue to trade with them, but that from now on I would pay cash for everything. My cash would provide for future provisions, but it would not settle the old debt. So it is, that you can quit your sin today, and if you never committed another sin, there is still an old account against you which is as black as midnight, and your reformation will never take care of this old debt. The only way to settle the debt is through the blood of Christ. You can come to him, and his righteousness will be placed to your account. Then you can truly say, "The old account was settled long ago." Reformation never does bring about the new birth, but the new birth will bring about reformation. When a man has been born again, he will immediately seek to straighten out his life.

2. The New Birth Is Not a Loud Profession

There is a difference between "profession" and "possession." Judas made a loud profession, but he never possessed eternal life. We are told that "he was a devil from the beginning" and that "he went to his own place." He fell from his role as apostle, but he never fell from grace, for he never had any grace. Many people today make loud profession, and we take them into the church, but this doesn't mean that they have been born again. You can fool men with a loud profession, but you cannot fool God. He looks upon the heart and listens not to the words of the lips.

3. The New Birth Is Not Joining the Church

Every saved man ought to join the church, but he ought to be saved before he joins. Joining the church will not save anybody. The church is not our Saviour; it is simply the home of the saved. If you say that you can live just as well outside the church, you are reflecting upon the wisdom of One who loved the church and gave himself for it. On the other hand, you can join all the churches in the world and submit to all their creeds, but this doesn't mean that you have been born again.

Reformation—church membership and profession, good works and baptism, culture and morality—does not save.

These things do not constitute regeneration, they are the results of it.

4. The New Birth Is a Divine Change

A man must be born of the Spirit—and that means that he must be born from above. It must be a change that comes from God and not from man. Man can persuade, but only God can create the divine change. Jeremiah 13: 23: "Can the Ethiopian change his skin, or the leopard his spots? then may ye also do good, that are accustomed to do evil." We are not able of ourselves to create this change, but when we repent of our sins and put our faith in Christ, God sends the change into our lives. But he must create the desire, and he must bring about the change.

5. The New Birth Is a Mysterious Change

Nicodemus said, "How can these things be?" and Jesus answered, "The wind bloweth where it listeth, and thou hearest the sound thereof, but canst not tell whence it cometh, and whither it goeth; so is every one that is born of the Spirit" (John 3:8). He is simply telling us that the new birth is a mystery which we can never fully understand. Yet there are mysteries all around us, and we accept them, although we cannot explain them. We cannot explain the mystery of electricity, but we trust it and use it. We cannot explain how the rainbow is hung on the dark clouds of the storm, but we enjoy it. We cannot explain how the gateway of the morn is pressed open and a new day is born, but we rejoice with every sunrise. We cannot explain how the sun falls upon a patch of dirt, thrilling it and causing it to bring forth a rose, but we enjoy the flowers. Explain all these things and then you will be able to tell how God sends the sunshine of his love into our darkened hearts, how he kisses the sin away, and how he brings forth the flower of truth and righteousness.

No man can fully understand this mystery which is called the new birth, but we can know this: that we are sinful, that we are lost without Christ, and that he can save us. We cannot understand the change, but, thank God, we can experience it.

6. The New Birth Is an Absolute Change

Second Corinthians 5:17: "Therefore if any man be in Christ, he is a new creature: old things are passed away; behold, all things are become new." Regeneration changes all things. We have new hopes, new ideals, new joys. The things which we once loved, we now hate, and the things which we once hated, we now love. The church of Christ, which we once despised, becomes to us the most beloved institution in the world, and the name of Christ, which once we used only profanely, becomes to us the sweetest sound of the human voice.

A man was converted one night in a revival meeting. The next morning, as he stood in the kitchen by the window, he looked out upon a brand-new world, and said to his wife, "Things look so different this morning—the grass is greener, and the trees are prettier, and the flowers are more beautiful than ever." The grass had not changed, and the trees and flowers had not changed, but this man had been changed, and all the world was different. Yes, the most radical change in all the world is the change that is caused by the new birth. It is indeed an absolute change.

II. THE NECESSITY OF THE NEW BIRTH

1. It Is Necessary Because We Are All Sinful

The garden of Eden story is re-enacted in every human life. We come to the crossroads as did Adam and

Eve. These crossroads are marked "obedience" and "disobedience." Each of us comes to the point of moral responsibility and moral accountability, and the tragedy of it is that we all walk down the wrong road because in everyone of us there is a tendency toward sin. And because we are all sinful—because we are all at enmity with God, we must be born again. We need a new birth out of sin and into favor with God and into the righteousness of the Lord Jesus Christ.

2. It Is Necessary Because We Are All Lost

Without the new birth we are eternally lost. "Except a man be born again, he cannot see the kingdom of God." When we are born into this world, we have a fleshly nature only; and flesh cannot inherit the kingdom of God. When we are born again of the Spirit, we receive a spiritual nature; and only the Spirit can inherit an eternal kingdom.

Ephesians 2:1: "You . . . were dead in trespasses and sins." In our natural state before God, we are dead, and before we can enter into the kingdom, we must be born again. This is one of the great imperatives of Jesus. We cannot get to heaven any other way—we must be born again.

III. How Is One Born Again?

1. God's Side

(1) *He calls us to himself.*—He calls in many ways. He calls through a sermon, or a song, or a sorrow. "The Spirit and the bride say, Come."

(2) *He convinces and convicts of sin.*—God is the One who causes us to have a feeling of lostness in our hearts. We can remember how he convinced and convicted us of our sins.

(3) *He brings repentance and faith.*

(4) *He puts away the believer's sin.*—He pronounces him justified, gives him a new nature and regenerates his soul. God is the agent in salvation. Preachers may preach and plead, but God is merely using them as his instruments. God is the One who convicts of sin, He is the one who brings man to himself. Often we hear someone say, "If that sermon doesn't bring people to Christ, I don't know what it will take to do it." No matter how strong or convincing the sermon may be, God must be the One who brings the conviction and the salvation.

John 6:44: "No man can come to me except the Father which hath sent me draw him." If we feel drawn to quit our sin and believe in Christ, we may know that God is drawing us. The tragic thing is that so many will not yield to the drawing power of the Spirit.

2. Man's Side

Does man do nothing about his own salvation? Some believe that they have only to sit and wait for salvation to come. This is not true—man's part is to receive and believe. God gives, but man receives, and unless man receives God's gift, he cannot be born again. John 1:12: "But as many as received him, to them gave he power to become the sons of God, even to them that believe on his name." Galatians 3:26: "For ye are all children of God by faith in Christ Jesus." It is clear from these scriptural passages that we are born into God's family through faith. If we trust Christ—if we ask God to forgive our sins because Jesus died for us—if we surrender our lives, our hearts, our all to him, immediately we will be born again.

Christ told Nicodemus all this, and then he drew a picture from the story of Israel. John 3:14: "And as Moses lifted up the serpent in the wilderness, even so must the Son of man be lifted up." When the Israelites were wandering in the wilderness after having sinned against God, the little fiery serpents stung them, and they were dying on every side. Moses asked God what to do about it, and God told him to lift a brazen serpent upon a pole, promising that every one who looked in faith to that serpent would be healed.

I can imagine this scene: One man who has looked, and who has been healed, goes to the tent of a sick friend and tells him all about it. The sick friend cries out: "It not use; my fever is high, my body is racked with pain, and I do not have the strength to look! Can't you see that I am dying?" "But," says his friend, "I know that this look will help you and heal you. I was just as far gone as you are, and I looked and was healed." Then he puts his strong arm under his friend and takes him to the door of the tent. "Now," he says, "look before it is too late." The man looks, and a new light comes into his eyes—he feels better in an instant—new life is coursing through his veins. "Why, I am better!" he says. "Look, my flesh is whole, I am all right again! Glory to God! I have been saved from death!"

Yonder is Jesus hanging upon a cross. I hear him say, "Look unto me, and be ye saved, all the ends of the earth." But a poor sinner says, "That is not for me, I am too far gone in sin." And the voice of Jesus comes to him saying, "Though your sins be as scarlet, they shall be as white as snow." The poor sinner looks—he is saved—he is born again—he is a child of God. Oh, how God must have loved us to provide such a wonderful salvation for us! And the beauty of it is that we can have it all when we repent of our sins and look unto him in faith.

IV. The Results of the New Birth

1. The Holy Spirit Comes to Dwell in Us

The minute that we are born again the blessed Third Person of the Trinity comes to dwell within our hearts. Before we are born again, we have no power to overcome sin, and we cannot understand spiritual things. When we are born again, and when the Spirit comes to live within us, he teaches us—he helps us to overcome temptation, he abides within us as a daily companion. First Corintians 6:19: "Your body is the temple of the Holy Spirit which is in you, which we have from God." One who is born again doesn't walk alone through the world; the Holy Spirit dwells with him as a loving friend.

2. Our Lives Are Transformed

Galatians 2:20: "I am crucified with Christ: nevertheless I live; yet not I, but Christ liveth in me: and the life which I now live in the flesh I live by the faith of the Son of God, who loved me, and gave himself for me." Zaccheus, the rich sinner, climbed a tree in order to see Jesus. When Jesus called him down out of this tree and told him that salvation had come to his house, Zaccheus said that he would sell half his goods and give the proceeds to the poor; also, that he would pay a fourfold portion to any man to whom he was indebted. His conversion made him right with God and with man. If your conversion did not go deep enough to transform your life it amounted to nothing.

A young man broke his mother's heart and wrecked his wife's life. He would get a job, but soon lose it through drinking and gambling. His family helped him out many times, but always he would drift back into the old sinful life. One day he said to a Christian friend, "I would like to go to South America and start life over again." The Christian answered, "The first person you would meet down there would be your old self—all the old habits and the old sins would be there with you. No outward condition, no new environment can help you. There is only one way in which you can win the victory, and that is through Jesus Christ the Lord. You must be born again." The Christian's message went like an arrow to the poor fellow's heart. He turned away in repentance from his sin and trusted Jesus Christ for salvation and for victory over sin. In a little while he was a new man, made over by the power of God. Only regeneration can transform our lives.

3. We Overcome the World

First John 5:4: "For whatsoever is born of God overcometh the world." The world is at variance with God. When we are born again, we can overcome the world because we have the strength and power of God on our side.

4. We Love Others

This is one sure mark of the new birth. If we do not love others, we have not been born again. First John 3: 14: "We know that we have passed from death unto life, because we love the brethren. He that loveth not his brother abideth in death."

5. We Confess Christ, We Obey Him, We Live for Him

If you have been born again, if your heart has been made right, you cannot help but confess Christ before men, obey him in baptism and follow him in church membership and live a good life for him day by day. "By their fruits ye shall know them." You may give many excuses for not confessing Christ and living for him, but the real reason is this: Your heart is wrong; you haven't been born again.

6. We Inherit Eternal Life

It is a fine thing to inherit a worldly fortune, but it is a more glorious thing to inherit eternal life. "Except a man be born again, he cannot see the kingdom of God." Don't you want to see heaven and all the glory and sweetness which it offers to your soul? You can never see it until you have been born again. You can see the great things of the world, but not the wonderful things of heaven unless you have been born again. You can see the great redwood trees of California, but you will never see the tree of life which grows near the throne of God unless you have been born again. You may see the beautiful rivers of the world, but you will never see the crystal river of life in heaven unless you have been born again. You may see the different countries of the world in all their varied beauty, but you will never see the "land that is fairer than day" unless you have been born again. You may see the great cities of the world, but you will never see the holy city of the New Jerusalem, whose builder and maker is God, unless you have been born again. You may live in the finest houses of this world, but you will never dwell in the "house of many mansions" unless you have been born again. You may receive degrees from many institutions, but unless you have received God's B.A. degree—God's Born Again degree— you will never enter into the Heavenly City.

Some years ago I was taken through one of the largest paper mills in the South. My guide took me to the place where the process of paper making began. I saw dirty, muddy logs thrown into a great machine and there torn apart and crushed to bits by the heavy teeth of the machinery. I saw the filthy juice flow out from this machine and then flow from one vat to another in the process of paper making. As the stream flowed on, I saw various chemicals being poured into the stream, and soon I noticed that the stream was becoming whiter and whiter. All the impurities were cleansed out—the juice was becoming solidified, and soon I saw it rolling over many rollers and coming out at the other end as smooth white paper. What a miracle of science that is! It was the same old material, but it has been transformed by a magic touch, and the old dirty logs had become white paper to be used in taking the news to the world, in writing business and love letters, and taking prose and poetry to the minds of men thousands of miles away. Regeneration is like that.

Yes, my friends, I preach Christ to you today. He can make your life over. He can set your feet upon a rock. He can lead you into pathways of peace. He can give you power to overcome temptations. He can plant hope in your heart. He does all these things when you are born again.

My friends, if man can do that, God can do even more. The living God can take our lives which are rough and sinful and make them into lives of purity and beauty and grace—lives which can then be used to give the message of hope to all the world. Who will yield to Christ today? He has transformed millions. He has carried multitudes to glory spotless and clean. He will do the same for you if you will only surrender to him. "Ye must be born again."

7

THE ATONEMENT THROUGH THE BLOOD

And almost all things are by the law purged with blood; and without shedding of blood is no remission.—HEBREWS 9:22.

A gospel without the Bible doctrine of the atonement is not a real gospel. Without this doctrine Christianity is but a devil's substitute. Satan's greatest enemy is the blood of Christ. If the devil had his way, no man would ever stand to preach on the atonement through the blood. Satan tells us that we can be saved by our good works—by our reformation—by doing the best that we can. But he is eternally wrong. The only way for us to be saved is through the blood of Christ.

Men everywhere today are avoiding this great doctrine. They magnify the life, the teachings, and the character of Jesus and they leave out his death; they are not preaching "Christ and him crucified." They tell us to practice the Golden Rule—to take Jesus as our master example. They are wrong; salvation is only through the blood. If it were not for the blood, we would all be lost, without God and without hope in the world. Let us turn from all our human notions, and let us thank God for One who came down from Heaven's glory, who lived a stainless life, who bore our sins upon a cross and poured out his precious blood that we might forever live.

I. THE NECESSITY AND IMPORTANCE OF CHRIST'S DEATH AND SHEDDING OF BLOOD

1. His Death Is Mentioned More than 175 Times in the New Testament

The Bible is full of the death of Christ. There is more about it in the Four Gospels than about anything else. If you cut out the references in the Bible to his shed blood, you would have a Bible without a heart and a gospel without saving power.

2. He Became a Man for the Specific Purpose of Dying

Hebrews 2:14: "Forasmuch then as the children are partakers of the flesh and blood, he also himself likewise took part of the same; that through death he might destroy him that had the power of death, that is, the devil." The meaning here is plain. Christ was incarnated for the purpose of dying in our stead. He was born to die. His death was not a mere accident of human life but the supreme purpose of it. He became a man that he might die as a man for all men.

3. His Death Was a Known Fact in Heaven

One day Jesus took certain of his disciples to the top of a high mountain, and before their eyes he was transfigured and made brighter than any light on land or sea. The disciples were overcome, and fell upon their faces in fear before him. The glory of it was greater than any man could bear. Moses and Elijah came and stood by the side of Jesus. They formed a committee which had been sent down from God. And what did they talk about? Did they talk about the miracles of Christ? his earthly life? his plan of organization for the new church? No, they talked about the death which he was going to die in Jerusalem. The atonement must have been important if God was willing to send a committee down to earth to talk to his Son about it.

4. His Death Is the Central Theme of Heaven's Song

Up there they do not sing, "Shall We Gather at the River?"—they are already there. Up there they do not

sing, "In the Sweet By and By"—they are living in it now.
Up there they do not sing, "More Like the Master"—
they shall be like him in that day. Up there they do not
sing, "Day is Dying in the West"—they are living in a land
where day shall never die. What, then, is the theme of
their song? We are told in the fifth chapter of Revelation, verse twelve, that the redeemed hosts of heaven sing
the new song about the Lamb who was slain: "Worthy
is the Lamb that was slain to receive power, and riches,
and wisdom, and strength, and honour, and glory, and
blessing." Yes, the big song in heaven will be about the
atoning death and the shed blood of Christ. Nothing is
more important that the atonement through the blood.

II. WHAT WAS THE PURPOSE OF THE DEATH AND THE
     SHED BLOOD OF JESUS CHRIST?

1. He Died as a Vicarious Offering for Sin

The dictionary tells us that "vicarious suffering" is
"suffering in the place of another." Jesus, the perfect
righteous One, deserved to live, but he died in the place
of unjust, sinful men who deserved to die. Isaiah 53:5:
"But he was wounded for our transgressions, he was
bruised for our iniquities: the chastisement of our peace
was upon him; and with his stripes we are healed." First
Peter 3:18: "For Christ also hath once suffered for sins,
the just for the unjust, that he might bring us to God."

Several years ago a number of men were working in a
huge pit near Asheville, North Carolina. A landslide
one day killed seven of these men. One man who usually
worked in this pit stayed at home that day, and his
brother went to work in his place and died in his stead.
This is an illustration of one man dying in the place of
another, but it is not a good illustration of Christ's atonement. This man did not know that he was going to

die in the place of his brother, but Jesus did know that he was going to die in the place of lost sinners. The principle of one suffering for another is all around us in this world, but the supreme example is given in Jesus. Of all the men who have come into this world, he deserved most to live; but he died in the place of men who deserved to die because of their sin.

2. He Died as a Ransom for Many

Matthew 20:28: "Even as the Son of man came not to be ministered unto, but to minister, and to give his life a ransom for many."

What is a ransom? A rich man's son is captured by kidnapers, and they hold him until the rich man pays a price which they demand. This money is called "ransom" money. Well, sin has man in its power, but Christ died to redeem man from sin and to secure his release from the power of the law. The difference is right here, however: The rich man gives his money for one who loves him, and Jesus gave himself for those who had sinned and rebelled against him.

3. He Died as a Sin Offering

Isaiah 53:10: "Thou shalt make his soul an offering for sin." In the ninth chapter of Hebrews we are told about the Old Testament offerings. We read of how innocent blood was shed and how this blood was offered as an atonement for sin. Once each year the high priest would venture into the holy of holies and there he would make a blood offering for his sins and for the sins of the people. This chapter points to these various sacrifices and then tells us that "without shedding of blood is no remission [of sin]." Then we are told that Jesus shed his blood, and that sins are remitted in his name, and there is no pardon and no forgiveness outside the atoning blood of Jesus.

4. He Died as a Propitiation for Our Sins

God has a holy wrath because of sin. He is not angry at the sinner, but at the sin, which hurts him. God hates sin with all his might. How can that wrath be appeased? Can man do it? Can man pay enough? No, Christ must die, and his blood must become the thing which appeases the wrath of God. First John 4:10: "Herein is love, not that we loved God, but that he loved us, and sent his Son to be the propitiation for our sins."

The word "propitiate" means "to render favorable." We had lost favor with God through sin, and we were brought back into this favor through the blood of the Lord Jesus Christ. God's holiness causes him to have a hatred of sin—a hatred which must be manifested. But he has a real love for the sinner. His wrath for sin must strike somewhere; it must smite the sinner or his substitute. Thank God, Christ became that substitute for me. "All we like sheep had gone astray; we had turned everyone to his own way; and the Lord hath laid on him the iniquity of us all." But someone will say, "It looks wrong for God, the first person, to take the sin of man, a guilty second person, and put it on Christ, an innocent third person." But this isn't the case. Christ isn't a third person; he is God himself taking the sin of man upon himself. God the Father suffered in the body of God the Son. He expressed his hatred for sin and his love for man, not by punishing the sinner, but by taking man's sin upon himself. This is more than just—this is gracious and wondrous love.

5. He Died to Redeem Us from the Curse of the Law

Have you always kept the law? Have you always obeyed every one of the Ten Commandments? No, the Bible tells us that we are guilty, and our own hearts condemn us. Since we broke the law, we have come under the curse of a broken law. But Jesus in his matchless love became a curse for us. "Cursed is every one that hangeth on a tree." His death by crucifixion redeemed us from the curse that we deserved.

6. He Died as Our Passover Sacrifice

This is the same truth in another form. Christ's blood serves as a ground on which God passes over us and spares. us. First Corinthians 5:7: "For even Christ our passover is sacrificed for us." You recall the picture of that awful night in Egypt. The death angel was to fly over the land and take the life of the eldest child in every home where there was no blood upon the doorpost. When the death angel saw the blood, he passed over that fortunate home. There is only one way for God to pass over us and save us: He must see the blood. Is the blood of Christ on the doorpost of your soul today? He died to furnish you this passover. Under his blood you are safe forevermore. The sacrifice is ready, but it is up to you to get under the blood.

III. THE RESULTS OF THE ATONING DEATH OF JESUS CHRIST

We have seen the glorious purpose of his death, but the results are even more glorious. I can speak of them only in part.

1. A Propitiation Is Provided for the World

First John 2:2: "And he is the propitiation of our sins: and not for ours only, but also for the sins of the whole world." This means that the death of Christ is the basis upon which God deals in mercy with the world. This is the only ground on which God can deal with any man. But when the rankest sinner comes to him, God is ready to deal with him in a saving way. When a child does wrong, the father may permit the child's brother to take the punishment upon himself. In this way the father is dealing with the bad son in mercy through the elder brother. This is a slight picture of what God did for us in Christ Jesus.

2. We Attain Resurrection from the Dead Through the Atoning Blood

First Corinthians 15:22: "For as in Adam all die, even so in Christ shall all be made alive." All through this chapter Paul is talking about the resurrection of Christ and the resurrection of believers. The curse of death came through Adam, causing all of us to suffer physical death. However, those who are in Christ shall live again unto life eternal. Which shall be your resurrection? Will you rise to life or to death? It all depends upon the attitude that you take toward Christ who gives you this resurrection.

3. All Believers Have Forgiveness of Sins Through His Atoning Death

Ephesians 1:7: "In whom we have redemption through his blood, the forgiveness of sins, according to the riches of his grace." Our forgiveness has already been secured through the blood, but we appropriate it through our faith.

A preacher said to a dying woman, "Have you made your peace with God?" "No," she said. "Do you realize," he said, "that you are dying and that soon you must go out to face God and give an account of your life?" "Yes," replied the woman, "but I am not disturbed about that. I do not have to make my peace with God; Christ made that peace for me on Calvary nineteen hundred years ago. I am simply resting in the peace which he has already made." The woman was right—he has already made peace by his death, and all we need to do is to enter into this peace. His work is complete and perfect and needs no additions and no subtractions. "We have peace through his blood."

4. All Believers in Him Are Justified

Romans 5:9: "Much more then, being now justified by his blood, we shall be saved from wrath through him." Justification is more than forgiveness. Forgiveness is simply the putting away of our sins, but justification makes us as if we had never sinned. All the righteousness of Christ is credited to us when we are justified. In his death upon the cross he took my place, and when I accepted him, I became his own, and I am justified freely from all things. I am sinful here, but I will be spotless there. We are told that he will "present us spotless before the throne." What blessed news this is. But this is our portion because of his shed blood.

5. All Believers Can Enter Boldly into the Presence of God Because of His Death

There was a time when man could not enter into the presence of God. However, when Christ died upon the cross, the veil of the Temple was rent in twain from the top to the bottom, and we can go through his blood straight to the heart of God. When we think of our sin, and when we think of his holiness, we hesitate to approach God. But because of the blood which was shed, we can enter into his presence and cry out, "Abba, Father." We can pour out our hearts to him because of Christ's wondrous blood.

6. All Believers Live with Him Forever

When he shall come, whether we are asleep or awake, we shall live forever with him. If it were not for his death, we could never know that blessed state which is the hope of every Christian.

> When He shall come with trumpet sound,
>   Oh, may I then in Him be found;
> Dressed in His righteousness alone,
>   Faultless to stand before the throne.

You and I have sinned. Our sin would send us to hell—but the blood of Jesus Christ, His only begotten Son, furnishes the power which cleanses us from our sin and which turns us toward the heavenly Home.

> What can wash away my sin?
>   Nothing but the blood of Jesus.
> What can make me whole again?
>   Nothing but the blood of Jesus.
> Oh! precious is the flow,
>   That makes me white as snow;
> No other fount I know,
>   Nothing but the blood of Jesus.

What does the blood of Christ mean to you? Are you his? Are you under his blood? If not, in that last day the blood will not avail for you. If you come now, he will wash you white as snow and give you the hope of eternal life. A Christian may endure many hardships and much suffering in this world, but he would not take anything for the hope which is his because of Jesus.

A soldier lay dying upon the battlefield. A chaplain came up to him and said, "Young man, can I do anything for you?" The young man reached trembling fingers into his pocket and took out a picture and gave it to the chaplain. "This is my mother's picture," said the young man. "On the back of that picture you will find her address. I wish you would write her and tell her about my death, but, most of all, tell her that it was all well with me because I died trusting Jesus as my Saviour."

Oh, my friends, because of the atonement—because of the shed blood—this can be true of every one of us.

8

SANCTIFICATION, THE MOST MISUNDER-STOOD DOCTRINE IN THE BIBLE

And the very God of peace sanctify you wholly; and I pray God your whole spirit and soul and body be preserved blameless unto the coming of our Lord Jesus Christ.
—1 THESSALONIANS 5:23.

What is the most misunderstood doctrine in the Bible? It is not baptism, although there is much misunderstanding of this doctrine. Some think that baptism has some saving power, but it has absolutely none. It is an act of obedience. Baptism is an outward thing; salvation is an inward thing. Baptism presents a picture of Christ's experience—his death, burial, and resurrection. It presents a picture of the Christian's experience—his death to sin, the burial of "the old man" and of his being raised to "walk in newness of life."

The Lord's Supper is not the most misunderstood doctrine in the Bible. There are some who think that there is saving grace in the Lord's Supper, but it is another outward thing. A man can partake of this Supper every Sunday and still be far away from God. It is not even a time for fellowship and communion with others; it is a memorial meal given us by Christ to remind us of what he did on Calvary for us.

The divinity of Christ is not the most misunderstood doctrine in the Bible. The Bible teaches that Christ is the divine Son of God. If we believe the Bible at all, we must believe in the divinity of Christ. Atonement through the blood is not the most misunderstood doctrine in the Bible. One great preacher said, "There is no more power

in the blood of Christ than in the blood of a chicken."
But we believe that, because of his death upon the cross
and the shedding of his blood, he made peace with God
for us and purchased our eternal salvation. It is true
that

> There is a fountain filled with blood
> Drawn from Immanuel's veins;
> And sinners, plunged beneath that flood,
> Lose all their guilty stains."

The second coming of Christ is not the most misunderstood doctrine in the Bible. However, it is the most
ignored doctrine. When you read the Bible in the light
of the blessed hope, it will become a great truth shining
upon your pathway like a beacon light.

Sanctification is the most misunderstood doctrine in the
Bible. The term has been used so loosely by some
people as to cause others to shy away from it. Someone
says, "I am sanctified." He means that he has had an
experience which has made him perfect. But the world
looks upon him and knows that he is not perfect. The
term "sanctification" has often been connected with those
people who boast of their holiness—who claim they are
perfect—who talk in unknown tongues and who roll
upon the floor. No wonder it has been misunderstood by
sincere Christian people.

Some people hold to the idea of holy perfection. They
say that since their conversion they have had an experience called "the second blessing." They say that the old
nature was taken away and they can never sin again.
There is no basis for such an idea in the Word of God.
In Romans 7:24, Paul cried out, "Who shall deliver me
from the body of this death?" He was simply using an old-
time illustration to say that we carry around with us our
rotten, carnal natures just as long as we live, and that

we will be free from them only when we go home to be with Christ.

Romans 7:15: "For that which I do I allow not: for what I would, that do I not; but what I hate, that do I."

Romans 7:22-23: "For I delight in the law of God after the inward man: but I see another law in my members, warring against the law of my mind, and bringing me into captivity to the law of sin which is in my members."

Philippians 3:12: "Not as though I had already attained, either were already perfect: but I follow after, if that I may apprehend that for which also I am apprehended of Christ Jesus." No there isn't a perfect human being in all the world, but the sincere humble Christian keeps reaching outward and upward and onward to Christ.

Sanctification is threefold. Let us study these three aspects of the subject.

I. SANCTIFICATION IS THE ACT OF SETTING SOMEONE OR SOMETHING APART FOR GOD'S USE

Jeremiah 1:5: "Before I formed thee in the belly I knew thee; and before thou camest forth out of the womb I sanctified thee, and I ordained thee a prophet unto the nations."

Leviticus 8:10: "And Moses took the anointing oil, and anointed the tabernacle and all that was therein, and sanctified them." These two passages illustrate how both a person and an object were sanctified or set apart for God's use. Now the thing in which we are most interested is personal sanctification. Every Christian is immediately sanctified or set apart at the time of his conversion. He is set apart for God's use. There are many who do not yield to God's touch and therefore they cannot be used, but it is God's purpose to use them just the same.

When America entered World War II, her great automobile plants were changed from peacetime production to wartime production. Instead of making automobiles, they began to make planes and tanks. In other words, they were set apart for a new type of work; the entire purpose of their machines was changed. And so it is that when a man is saved, the purpose of his life is changed, and no longer is he to serve sin. He has been set aside to serve God.

Here is a man who works in an office. During the war he receives a letter from the President which begins with the one word, "Greetings." He answers this call of his country and is soon inducted into the army. His old life is suddenly changed; he has different clothes and different companions. No longer does he live in the bosom of his family; he is living among a group of total strangers. No longer is he sitting at a desk; he is out lugging his gun under the hot sun. He has been changed altogether; his life has been set apart for a new purpose.

So it is when a man is saved and sanctified—he, too, is changed altogether. God sends his greetings of love and mercy, calling him out of the world and setting him aside for a new purpose.

For many years the scientists were studying the matter of splitting the atom. They knew that there was power in the atom if they could just loose it and harness it. One day they found the secret, and now we have the atom bomb, the greatest exhibition of power in the world.

So it is that the Christian is possessed with the power of God. God has set him aside for his own use, and when he realizes his position and surrenders to the Lord and enters into the divine plan, this is the first meaning of sanctification. It is God's instantaneous act of setting one aside for his own use.

II. SANCTIFICATION IS A PROGRESSIVE WORK OF GROWTH IN GRACE

Second Peter 3:18: "But grow in grace, and in the knowledge of our Lord and Saviour Jesus Christ. To him be glory both now and for ever."

Second Corinthians 3:18: "But we all, with open face beholding as in a glass the glory of the Lord, are changed into the same image from glory to glory, even as by the Spirit of the Lord."

Paul pictures the Christian as a child and Jesus as a full-grown man. The child looks upon the man. He begins to grow as he looks, and some day he becomes like the grown man. This is the progressive idea of sanctification—the idea of growing in grace. Now just as certain things cause a child to grow, so there are certain means of spiritual growth.

1. The Study of God's Word Is a Means of Spiritual Growth

The Bible is a mirror. A woman looks into the mirror and sees her wrinkles, and she immediately sets about to correct the situation. We look in the Bible and see our sins. We find that we come short of the glory of God, and we set about to correct our lives. The Bible is a map. It is a lamp unto our feet. Some time ago a travel agency sent me a map on which they had outlined a trip for me from Florida to Canada. They had marked with red ink the road upon which I should travel. The Bible is also marked with a red line—with the red line of Christ's blood, showing us the way from sin to glory. The Bible is our food. You feed a baby properly and you have joy in watching him grow. And so it is if we feed on the Bible, we grow in grace.

A woman one day was dusting her books, one of which was her Bible. The little girl said, "Mother, is that God's Book?" The mother answered, "Yes." "Well," said the little girl, "why don't we send it back to God: we never do use it." No, we will never grow in grace unless we use the Bible.

2. Prayer Is a Means of Spiritual Growth

Prayer isn't so much asking things for ourselves as it is getting ourselves in a right attitude toward God and man. Prayer helps us to get sin out of our lives. When you pray, you look into the face of Christ. You thank him for his blessings, and you confess your sins. You want him to use you, and you ask him to make you usable.

One day you are invited to a meal in a friend's home. You sit down and look at the snowy white linen and the fine silver. You know that the food will be tasty and well-prepared, and you look forward to your meal. Then you look down at your plate and you find that it is filthy—it is covered with the remains of the former meal. Your appetite is soon gone and you do not want any of the food served to you. Well, lost souls are hungry for the Bread of life. They are looking to us for it, and if our lives are unclean, if there are wrong things in them, the world wants none of that thing which we call Christianity. Now, prayer helps us to keep our lives clean and promotes growth in grace.

3. Faithfulness to Duty Is a Means of Spiritual Growth

There is a technique in building a skyscraper or an airplane or a ship. There is also a technique in building a Christian character, and faithfulness is a big part of the technique. We ought to be faithful in church attendance. I challenge you to show me a person who has grown in grace if he has not been faithful in attending his church. The preacher is hurt when his people absent themselves from God's house, because he knows that they are missing a great aid to spiritual growth. We ought to be faithful in our stewardship. Our time, our talents, and our tithe belong to God and we will never grow in grace unless we give them to him in full measure.

Robert E. Lee said that "duty is the sublimest word in the English language." You cannot turn your back upon what you know to be your duty without bringing some harm to your spiritual life. If you see a thing that you ought to do—a thing which you know is of God—and if you refuse to do that thing, something dies within you. "To him that knoweth to do good, and doeth it not, to him it is sin."

You stand by a blind man upon the curb of the street. It is your duty to lead the man through the traffic and across the street. You fail to do this, and immediately you have killed something good within yourself. A warm glow fills your heart if you do that which is your duty. So it is, if you do your duty as a Christian, you bring something good into your own life. Tithing is a part of your duty to God. What is more destructive to good character than dishonesty? Surely if a man steals from God, he will never grow in grace.

4. Looking Up to Jesus is Another Means of Spiritual Growth

Dr. E. C. Sheridan tells an interesting story about Dr. John Roach Straton, former pastor of the Calvary Baptist Church, of New York City. When Straton was a little boy, he and his brothers decided to have some fun at the expense of Aunt Millie, their faithful old Negro mammy. One night they secured a pumpkin, hollowed it out, cut holes in it for eyes, and formed a mouth with jagged teeth. In the darkness they went down to Aunt Millie's cabin, put the pumpkin upon a post, lighted the candle within it and wrapped a bed sheet around the post. They then slipped to the cabin window and started to rap upon the shutter. They were going to enjoy Aunt Millie's fright when she saw the "ghost" in her yard. But they heard a voice inside the cabin and looked through the crack to see who was there with Aunt Millie. Instead of seeing someone else, they saw Aunt Millie down on her knees in prayer. The light of the moon was shining upon her big black face as it was lifted heavenward. They heard her pray for the "Missus" who was sick in the big house. They heard her call every boy by name as she prayed to God for them. They remembered then how she had cared for them all their lives—how she had comforted them when they had had trouble with their father. They remembered how she had watched over their mother day and night while she was sick, sleeping through many nights on the floor right by her bed. The boys did not scare Aunt Millie that night. They slipped away from the cabin, taking the pumpkin and the bed sheet with them, went to their rooms and fell upon their knees in prayer. Soon they were in bed, sobbing themselves to sleep. John became a great preacher, but he said that he never was able to get away from this picture of devotion, and that every time he thought of Aunt Millie and her prayers it made him a better man.

Oh, let me tell you something greater! If we look into the face of the Lord Jesus Christ, we are moved and inspired to become more like him. Yes, growth in grace is another part of sanctification.

III. Sanctification Reaches Its Final Stage At Christ's Second Coming

First John 3:2 "Beloved, now we are the sons of God, and it doth not yet appear what we shall be: but we know that, when he shall appear we shall be like him; for we shall see him as he is." First Corinthians 15:52: "In a moment, in the twinkling of an eye, at the last trump: for the trumpet shall sound, and the dead shall be raised incorruptible, and we shall be changed." First Corinthians 15:49: "And as we have borne the image of the earthy, we shall also bear the image of the heavenly." Philippians 1:6: "Being confident of this very thing, that he which hath begun a good work in you will perform it until the day of Jesus Christ."

When we are saved, we are sanctified: we are set aside for God's use. If we grow in grace, the process of sanctification is going on within us. But when Jesus comes again, our sanctification will be complete and we shall be perfect, for we shall be like him. Oh, what a change will come to us when Jesus comes again! Some Christians will be in their graves, and some will be living in this old cruel world, but the heavens will open, the Lord will descend with a shout, with the voice of the archangel and with the trump of God, and we shall then go up to meet him, and in the twinkling of an eye we shall be completely changed. If he did not change us, we would all be out of place in God's perfect home.

First, it will be a physical change. We will have a new body, and all the aches and pains will be gone. Then it will be a mental change—all God's mysteries will be as clear as light. "Now we see through a glass darkly; but then face to face: now I know in part; but then I shall know even as also I am known." It will be a spiritual change—we will be absolutely perfect in every way. This is God's ultimate salvation. It is not complete when we are saved nor when we die, but when Jesus comes again. Romans 8:29-30: "For whom he did foreknow, he also did predestinate to be conformed to the image of his Son, that he might be the firstborn among many brethren. Moreover whom he did predestinate, them he also called: and whom he called, them he also justified: and whom he justified, them he also glorified."

All the way from ages past through the ages to come, on into eternity, God plans and labors to save and to sanctify us and to make us over into his likeness and to take us to his spiritual home. In Adam paradise was lost—in Christ paradise is forever regained.

A young man lay upon a hospital bed. He had been hurt in an accident. He wasn't a Christian. He did not know how serious his injury was, but he knew he was in very great pain. Suddenly everything was changed. A nurse came quickly into the ward and put a screen around his bed. He knew what that meant—they expected him to die. His whole world began to collapse around him. He heard the clock chime. He told himself that he would probably be dead before it chimed again. His life began to pass before his eyes. He had lived without God, and now the crushing weight of his sin settled upon him. He trembled as he thought of meeting God. His eyes wandered above the screen, and there upon the opposite wall suddenly the answer came to him, for on that wall was a Scripture motto which said, "Come unto me, all ye that labour and are heavy laden, and I will give you rest."

That was it—these were the words of Jesus. Somehow he remembered that a fellow could be saved if he came to Christ. He remembered the pictures that he had seen of Christ with outstretched arms inviting sinners to come to him. He knew that Jesus had a pardon waiting for all those who accepted his invitation. He read the Scripture passage over several times, and then, with deep emotion, he said from the depths of his heart: "I will come! I do come! I do come to thee? Is it too late?" The man in the next bed heard him and said, "Poor fellow, he is delirious." The man behind the screen was smiling now. He was happy—he had a Saviour, and he was ready to die. He only wished that he could live a little longer in order that he might tell his brothers and his friends about Christ. Then the nurse come back and removed the screen. "I am sorry, sir," she said, "there has been a mistake. I put the screen around the wrong bed. I am very, very sorry, sir." But to her great astonishment the patient sat up in the bed and cried out: "Sorry! Why, that is the greatest thing that ever happened to me!"

Oh, friend, come to Jesus, and it will be the greatest thing that has ever happened to you. He will save you and sanctify you and satisfy you, and some day he will glorify you. Hallelujah, what a Saviour!

9

JUSTIFICATION BY FAITH

Being justified freely by his grace through the redemption
that is in Christ Jesus.—ROMANS 3:24.

Therefore we conclude that a man is justified by faith without the deeds of the law.—ROMANS 3:28.

In the year 1512 a young man by the name of Martin
Luther was serving as a professor in the University of
Wittenberg. He was a man of deep religious convictions.
He had entered the monastery of the Roman Catholic
Church and had now been made a university professor.
The day came when young Luther was sent to Rome to
transact some business with the pope. He joyfully be-
gan his journey, believing that his church was supreme
and that the pope was the incarnation of perfection and
absolutely infallible.

When Martin Luther arrived in Rome and found such
corruption in the church, he was greatly upset. His faith
in an infallible church was being tremendously shaken.
Feeling himself to be sinful and rebellious, he made his
way to the cathedral and began climbing the Scala
Sancta, the "sacred stairs." As he climbed the stairs he
kissed each step as was the custom. In a few minutes a
verse of Scripture began to ring out in his memory, "The
just shall live by faith—the just shall live by faith." After
serious reflection and consideration, Martin Luther re-
nounced his connection with the Catholic Church and
went out to preach the doctrine of justification. "The just
shall live by faith," he said, "not by works, nor by
penance, but by faith." This same doctrine had been

preached many years before by the apostle Paul, but it had been lost in the mystic maze of a ceremonial religion. Now the doctrine began to live again and out of Martin Luther's experience there came the Reformation and the Protestant church with its distinctive doctrines.

Luther's text is found in four different books of the Bible. It is in Hebrews 10:38; Habbakuk 2:4; Romans 1:17; and Galatians 3:11. These passages do away forever with the belief that man is saved by anything except his faith in Jesus Christ.

I. What Is Justification?

It is the act by which God declares a sinner just and righteous, as if he had never sinned. It is more than a pardon; a pardon frees merely from the penalty of sin but not from the guilt of sin. Justification frees from all guilt and blame.

Here is a man who has committed a crime against the state. The governor pardons this man, but he is still guilty of his crime. In justification God not only pardons the sinner but declares him innocent and justified. In one of our states a certain man refused a pardon which the governor offered to him. He stated that he was innocent of any crime and told the governor that he wanted more than a pardon—he wanted the governor to declare him as being entirely innocent. That is what God does—not only does he free the soul from the penalty of sin—not only does he save him from hell, but he makes him as if he had never sinned. Justification, therefore, frees a man completely and entirely from the guilt of his sin.

When a sinful soul comes in faith to Jesus Christ, God declares him righteous as if he had never sinned. He becomes absolutely spotless in the sight of God. Oh, this is a glorious doctrine which makes us just and righteous before a high and holy God!

II. The Need of Justification

Who needs justification? All of us need it. Romans 3: 23: "All have sinned, and come short of the glory of God." Romans 3:10: "There is none righteous, no, not one." If all of us have sinned, if all of us are unrighteous, then all of us need justification. You and I and every person in all the world need justification.

III. How Are Men Justified?

1. They Are Not Justified by Works

They are not justified by living a good moral life, nor by keeping the law, nor by following the Golden Rule, nor by performing charitable deeds. Galatians 2:16: "Knowing that a man is not justified by the works of the law, but by the faith of Jesus Christ, even we have believed in Jesus Christ, that we might be justified by the faith of Christ, and not by the works of the law: for by the works of the law shall no flesh be justified." Ephesians 2:8-9: "For by grace are ye saved through faith; and that not of yourselves: it is the gift of God: not of works, lest any man should boast." Romans 3:20 "Therefore by the deeds of the law there shall no flesh be justified in his sight: for by the law is the knowledge of sin."

You may live the best life in the world—sell all that you have and give it to the poor—do unto others as you would have them do unto you—observe the law right down to the letter, and yet you will not be justified in God's sight. "The just shall live by faith," not by works.

2. They Are Not Justified by Performing Religious Duties

A man isn't justified by offering prayers, by doing penance, by joining the church, by church attendance, by baptism or the Lord's Supper. Our works don't save us; we are saved by the works of another. We are saved by the death of the Lord Jesus Christ on Calvary's cross. We are justified through his death, and all who come and appropriate him to themselves by faith are entirely justified.

3. They Are Justified as a Free Gift of God

Romans 3:24: "Being justified freely by his grace through the redemption that is in Christ Jesus." Too many people are trying to pay for their salvation; but the free gift of God bestows salvation upon man. It is hard to make man understand that salvation costs nothing. God gives unto us eternal life. If we pay him for this life, he is not giving us anything. We do not mean by this that salvation costs nothing. It did cost Someone everything that he had. It cost Jesus Christ his life blood, but he gives it to us as a free gift.

A preacher tried to explain to a miner that salvation is a free gift of God. The miner could not understand it in this way. One day the preacher accompanied him to the mines. They were preparing to descend several hundred feet by means of the company elevator, when the preacher said to the miner, "How much will this cost me?" The miner replied, "It will cost you nothing." The preacher then said, "That is too cheap; I don't want to ride on anything that cost nothing." "Cheap!" exclaimed the miner. "This elevator cost $25,000—the company paid that much for it." "Oh," said the preacher, "I understand—it cost me nothing but it did cost someone else a great price." So he was able to explain to the miner that salvation came to us in the same manner. It costs us nothing, but it did cost Another a great price— it cost Christ all that he had. Justification, therefore, originated up yonder in the great loving heart of God. It then flows down through Calvary and through Jesus Christ to the heart of man.

4. They Are Justified Through the Blood of Jesus Christ

Romans 5:9: "Much more then, being now justified by his blood, we shall be saved from wrath through him." We are counted righteous through his blood that was shed upon Calvary. We were under the curse, but he redeemed us by his blood. We deserved to die, but he took our place before God—took upon himself all the penalty of a broken law, and now we are counted righteous because of him. The one and only ground for our justification is the blood of Jesus Christ.

"All we like sheep have gone astray," but Jesus offered his blood as an atonement for our sin. God accepted this offering. He was satisfied with the price that was paid, and through the blood of Jesus Christ we become justified in God's sight.

5. They Obtain Justification Through Faith in Jesus

Romans 4:5 "But to him that worketh not, but believeth on him that justifieth the ungodly, his faith is counted for righteousness." Romans 3:28: "Therefore we conclude that a man is justified by faith without the deeds of the law." If we believe in Jesus Christ as our Saviour, our faith brings justification down to us. God is asking only that we believe in his Son. If we do, it is counted unto us for righteousness. The question then becomes not, What works do you have to offer, but Have you appropriated Christ and his blessings unto yourself by faith? We are justified, not by our works, but by his. We are proud people, and we want to pay the price for salvation, but we cannot do it—it is absolutely free. When a man repents of his sins and accepts Jesus Christ by faith, he is justified forever.

(1) *Such faith brings confession.*—Romans 10:9-10: "That if thou shalt confess with thy mouth the Lord Jesus, and shalt believe in thine heart that God hath raised him from the dead, thou shalt be saved. For with the heart man believeth unto righteousness; and with the mouth confession is made unto salvation."

The faith which does not bring confession isn't a faith which brings salvation and justification. You may have a mere opinion in your mind about Jesus Christ, but if this opinion does not bring about action, it is not a justifying faith. A man said to me one day, "Why, even the devil believes in Jesus." But this isn't the kind of faith that justifies. If your heart is right, if you are justified by faith, you are not ashamed to confess Christ as your Saviour. You are happy to follow him in baptism, in a good life, and in church membership.

(2) *Such faith brings forth good fruit.*—James 2:14: "What doth it profit, my brethren, though a man say he hath faith, and have not works? Can faith save him?" The faith which a man merely says that he has but which doesn't cause him to work for Christ is a faith that doesn't save. It takes real faith to save a sinner, and this real faith will lead to confession and to good works. We are justified upon the single, simple condition of real faith in Jesus Christ. But if this faith is real—if you have been justified—you will confess him as Saviour and your life will bear Christian fruits. If your faith does not produce these things, it is not a real faith; it is not a justifying faith.

IV. How Does Justification Work?

1. It Is an Instantaneous Act

When I first moved to the city, I lived with a family which had an instantaneous gas heater in the bathroom. When I lighted this gas heater, I could then turn on the water and find it to be warm. I did not have to wait thirty minutes for it to warm up. Justification is like that. The very minute we are saved, we are justified. It is not a progressive act. When you have been born again, immediately you are justified before God.

A woman said to me once, "I had to go the mourner's bench a week before I could be saved." Well, it would take a sinner much longer than that to save himself, but Christ can save you in a second and justify you immediately. There are two lines in the chorus of an old song which illustrate this fact.

> Only trust Him, only trust Him,
> Only trust Him now.

The emphasis is on the word "now." The second line says:

> He will save you, He will save you,
> He will save you now.

The emphasis is still on the word "now." When you trust Christ, he saves you. All who accept Christ as Saviour are justified in that very minute.

The judge yonder in the court speaks to a man and says, "I declare you innocent; you are hereby acquitted." This doesn't mean that the man must languish in jail for a week or two—he is immediately released. So it is with God. When we believe, he declares us not only saved, but justified.

Acts 13:39: "And by him all that believe are justified from all things, from which ye could not be justified by the law of Moses." We are not going to be justified, but we are justified when we come to Christ.

Let the vilest sinner in all the world come to Jesus Christ, and in that very moment his sins will be blotted out. He will become justified, and all the perfect righteousness of Christ will be his. His standing before God will be just the same as if he had been in heaven for ten million years.

Pope Gregory and Henry IV of Germany had some differences between themselves. The pope excommunicated the king and made him ineligible to sit upon the throne. The king came to Rome to do penance and to seek absolution. He found that the pope was away in the mountains. The king then went to the mountains and stood outside the pope's cabin in the snow all the night long. The next morning he received "absolution" from the pope.

It isn't that way with our God. When we approach him through Jesus Christ, we do not have to wait for our forgiveness. He forgives us and justifies us in the very second when we come to him through Christ.

2. It Is an Irreversible Act

The law doesn't hold a man in jeopardy the second time for the same crime. A man kills another man in self-defense. The jury acquits the man of his crime and frees him from all guilt, and never again is that man in danger of the law for this same crime. And so it is that when God declares us justified, no one can change the verdict. All the devils in hell may assail our soul, but that cannot reverse this great act of justification.

3. It Is an Unpurchasable Act

A dying man may want to do something to merit salvation. He therefore leaves his money to some church or good cause, hoping thus to merit the favor of God, but you cannot buy salvation. A sinner may give a million dollars to the cause of Christ, but this will not buy his way into the kingdom of God.

A man knocks upon the door of a certain home. He is dressed in good clothes, and the diamonds are sparkling upon his fingers. When the man of the house opens the door, this man says, "I am hungry, and I thought that if I would fix myself up, I could commend myself unto you." This certainly would not cause the man of the house to give food to the other man. But if he came to the door ragged and starving and begged for bread, the man of the house would gladly give unto him. You can go to God's door and brag about your goodness and righteousness and make a plea for salvation, and God is forced to say "No" to you. "I came not to call the righteous, but sinners to repentance," says Jesus. Never did one ever come to him as a beggar and a poor lost sinner but that Christ took him in. He came to save sinners, but salvation and justification are free, and no man can buy them.

V. The Blessings of Justification

1. Justification Brings a Full and Free Pardon

It is a pardon which covers all sin, past, present, and future. When a man accepts Christ, he is justified. He has a pardon for every sin committed from the hour of birth to the hour of death. Men limit God when they say that he saves men and justifies them and then permits them to go to hell because of some sin that is committed. He doesn't save on the instalment plan; when we come to Him through Christ, we are his, and we are justified eternally.

2. Justification Produces Perfect Standing with God

Sin has marred our standing with God. It has come between us and him, but through justification we can stand blameless before God. When we look through a red glass, all objects look alike. When God looks at us through the law, he sees the black sin that is within us. But when he looks at us through the blood of Christ, he sees us as sinless and perfect.

When we are justified we take our standing with God, not as a servant, but as a son. "You are not hired as a servant, but you are born into the royal family" and you become a joint heir with Christ of all the good things of heaven.

3. Justification Brings Peace with God

Romans 5:1: "Therefore being justified by faith, we have peace with God through our Lord Jesus Christ." Martin Luther had no peace when he did penance on the sacred stairs. He knew the peace of God when he had been justified. It is the peace which the world cannot give and which the world cannot take away.

Are you troubled on the inside? Are you anxious, not knowing what will happen to you when you die? Then come to Jesus, and he will indeed give to you "the peace that passeth all understanding."

Venice is a city of waterways and canals. Over one of these canals there is a bridge called "The Bridge of Sighs." This bridge leads from a courtroom to a dismal prison. In this prison guilty criminals are left to rot and die. Written over the door of the prison are these words, "Abandon hope, all ye who enter here." I can imagine a man being led across this bridge. He has kissed his loved ones good-by. He is looking into the sunlight for the last time. His heart is filled with grief and despair.

When he is halfway across the bridge, a court attendant rushes up to him and cries out ,"Halt! I have here a complete pardon for you." Can you imagine the happiness and joy which flood the soul of this man? He straightens up his shoulders, and a new light comes into his eyes. Now he is free. Now he can go home and enjoy life with his loved ones and his friends. He has in his possession a pardon which has set him free.

Oh, my friends, this is a slight illustration of what God can do for a man who is doomed because he has broken God's law. The sinner without Christ is on his way to death—no hope shines across the pathway for him. And then one day he looks to the Saviour upon the cross. He hears a voice say unto him, "Do you believe?" And with all his heart he cries out, "I do believe—I do believe in Jesus Christ, and I accept him as my Saviour." That minute—that very minute he is free—he is saved—he is justified. His soul is flooded with happiness and joy. His sins are forgiven, and he stands before God as one of his children. Hell and eternal suffering are forever abolished so far as he is concerned. He is walking with the Lord, and he is going home to heaven.

Don't you want this great salvation and this marvelous justification to be yours? You can have it because of One who died upon Calvary's cross for you and for me. Come and give your heart to Him today.

10

THE SECOND COMING OF CHRIST

For the Lord himself shall descend from heaven with a shout, with the voice of the archangel, and with the trump of God: and the dead in Christ shall rise first: then we which are alive and remain shall be caught up together with them in the clouds, to meet the Lord in the air; and so shall we ever be with the Lord.—1 THESSALONIANS 4:16-17.

This old world has seen some great days. It was a great day when God created the heavens and the earth and all the things they contain. It was a great day when God sent the flood upon the earth to destroy the sinful civilization that had sprung up. It was a great day when Jesus was born, and the angel of the Lord said, "Unto you is born this day in the city of David a Saviour, which is Christ the Lord." It was a great day when that same Saviour hung upon the cross and bled his life away for you and me. It was a great day when he conquered death and the grave and came back to live forevermore. It was a great day when he ascended on high to take his place at the right hand of the throne of God. But there shall come another great day—a day filled with power and glory and blessing—the day when Jesus Christ shall come again. The most glorious fact of the past is this, Jesus came to save sinners and died upon the cross for lost men. The grandest fact of the future is this, Jesus is coming back again.

I. THE CERTAINTY OF HIS COMING

1. The Bible Teaches Us that He Is Coming Again

We are told in the Bible scores of times that the Lord Jesus is coming back. We look at the scene yonder on

Mount Olivet. He is having his last conversation with his friends and disciples. He breathes a blessing upon them. He gives them a new commission and tells them good-by for a while. A cloud comes down out of heaven and surrounds him. He ascends in that cloud, going up and up and up until he is out of sight. The disciples stand there speechless in open-mouthed amazement. In a moment they are surprised to see two men in white standing near them. These men speak out to them and say, "Why stand ye here gazing into heaven? this same Jesus which is taken up from you into heaven, shall so come in like manner as ye have seen him go into heaven" (Acts 1:11).

The Bible always proves itself. It tells us that a flood was coming, and the flood did come. It tells us that Jesus was coming into the world, and he did come. It tells us that he is coming again the second time, and he will come. For thousands of years the prophets pointed toward one thing—the first coming of Christ. When he did come, they did not recognize him because they thought he was coming as a king, and instead he came as the poorest of the poor. There are 318 references in the New Testament to the second coming of Christ. Just as he fulfilled prophecy in his first coming, so will he fulfil it again in his second coming.

2. The Lord's Supper Points to His Coming

Jesus instituted the Lord's Supper, which points two ways: it points backward to the cross and forward to his coming again. First Corinthians 11:26: "For as often as ye eat this bread, and drink this cup, ye do shew the Lord's death till he come." The Lord's Supper points backward to his death and forward to his descent from heaven—it points to the blood-stained cross and to the gilded throne. When we partake of the Lord's Supper, we say to ourselves, "I believe that he has come, and I am looking forward to his coming again." Perhaps some congregation will be partaking of the Lord's Supper when he comes. The shout, "Behold, the bridegroom cometh," will fill the air. It will not be necessary then to partake of the Lord's Supper any more, for all the Christians in the world will be caught up to meet him face to face.

3. Jesus Said He Was Coming Back

Yonder in the upper room, as he talked to the sorrowing disciples, he told them that he was leaving them for a while but that he would be coming back. He said, "I will come again, and receive you unto myself; that where I am, there ye may be also." Every word that Jesus said is true. He said that he would die and rise again on the third day, and so he did. He said that he was coming back some day, and so he will. The second coming of Christ is the greatest certainty of the future.

II. The Manner of His Coming

1. Let Us Look at It from the Negative Standpoint

(1) *Conversion is not the second coming of Christ.*--There are some who believe that when we are converted, this is the second coming of Christ. Well, Paul had Jesus in his heart after conversion, and yet he looked for his coming. John had Jesus in his heart, and yet he said, "Even so, come, Lord Jesus." We are told that when Jesus comes, there will be a shout—the voice of the archangel and the trump of God. At that time all living Christians will be caught up out of the world and all dead Christians shall rise up to meet him. This does not happen at conversion, so we know that conversion is not the second coming of Christ.

(2) *The coming of the Holy Spirit is not the second coming.*—We are told about the coming of the Holy Spirit in the second chapter of Acts. But after that time there are 150 references to the second coming of Christ. The Holy Spirit is here now, but Jesus is yet to come.

(3) *The spread of the gospel is not the second coming.*—Preachers have gone up and down the world preaching Christ for many years. The old, old story has been translated into a thousand languages. The message of Christ is known in every part of the globe, but this is not the second coming of Christ.

(4) *Progress in humanitarian enterprises is not the second coming.*—Some people point to the hospitals and the orphanages and the homes for the aged, and they say, "That is what Christ meant when he said he was coming back." No, these things are the outgrowth of Christianity; they are the fruits of faith. This is not the personal return of the Lord.

(5) *Death is not the second coming of Christ.*—When the Christian dies, he can truthfully say, "The Lord has come for me." But death is not the second coming of Christ, for death is just opposite to the second coming of Christ. Death is our worst enemy, but his coming means the coming of our best Friend. After his coming, there will be no more death for us, for death will be swallowed up in victory.

My mother died when I was a little boy. She was a good Christian, and I know that the Lord came for her, but this did not literally mean the second coming of Christ. There was no shout from the heavens when she died. The graves of the saved were not opened up when she died, and none of the living Christians were caught up into heaven when she died. Death is not the second coming of Christ.

2. Now Let Us Look at It from the Positive Standpoint

(1) *His coming will be personal.*—In Acts 1:11 we are told, "This same Jesus" will return. His going away was personal, and his coming back will be personal. We read in our text that "the Lord himself" will return. It seems that the Holy Spirit put the word "himself" in this verse for emphasis. Yes, one day he is coming. You may be at church—you may be at work—you may be asleep. God grant that you will be ready when he makes his personal appearance.

When a relative goes away, you say to him, "Come again soon." One day he comes back to your home. You don't imagine that he is coming—you don't just feel that maybe he will come. He does come in person, and you rejoice to see him. Jesus said, "I am coming again." Therefore when we look for him, we are looking for a personal coming.

(2) *His coming will be sudden.*—"In such an hour as ye think not the Son of man cometh." A Scotch preacher said to a group of people one day, "Do you think that Jesus will come today?" And they said, "No, we think not." And the preacher replied, "In an hour that you think not the Son of man cometh."

When Noah was expecting the flood, he went ahead building the ark and preaching to the people. Those who looked on were not looking for a flood. They went about their daily living in the usual way, eating and drinking, marrying and giving in marriage. And then one day suddenly the flood came just as God had promised it would, and those who had laughed at the idea perished beneath the waters. Today there are thousands of people who pay no attention to the matter of the second coming of Christ. There are many who even laugh at the idea, but some day he will come suddenly even as he has promised. Woe, then, unto all those who have not Christ as their Saviour!

(3) *His coming will be twofold.*—I believe that if we can get this idea in our minds, we will be able to understand more fully the scriptural teaching concerning his coming. He will come first in the air. At that time he will not come down to earth but will stop somewhere in the upper air. At that time the dead in Christ shall rise up to meet him. The living Christians will be caught up in the air together with them, and all of them shall be transformed and made like unto Christ. This great company, with Jesus leading them, will move into heaven.

In the other part of his coming, he will descend to the earth in glory. This will be after the tribulation period. He will come back to the world and bring all his people with him. His feet shall stand upon the Mount of Olives. He will destroy the Antichrist—lock up the devil and reign with the saints upon the earth for a thousand years. Later he will raise the wicked dead, and they and the devil will be cast into the lake of fire. The eternal ages will then begin. Christ will be in heaven with his own, and the devil will be in hell with his own.

Now let us get this right. The Bible doesn't teach the idea of one general judgment. There are some who say that when Jesus comes, he will gather all people before him and judge them, sending some to the right and some to the left. This is not according to the Bible at all. There are two phases of his coming: He will come in the air and take his saved ones up with him. He will come in glory and overcome the world. He will come the first time for his saints. He will come the second time and bring his saints with him.

III. The Time of His Coming

1. No Man Knows the Exact Time of His Coming

The time-setters are mistaken; they have no authority for pointing out the time when Christ will come. A few years ago a New Jersey man announced that Christ would come on a certain morning at sunrise. His followers went with him to a high hill to wait for Jesus, but he did not come. In England another man announced that Christ was coming on a certain day. He and his followers on that day were clothed in their white ascension robes and were waiting for Christ, but he did not come. Oh, my friends, the only robe which we will need on that day will be the robe of righteousness of our Lord and Saviour Jesus Christ. But we cannot tamper with God's timetable. We do not know when he is coming.

Acts 1:7: "And he said unto them, It is not for you to know the times or the seasons, which the Father hath put in his own power."

Mark 13:32: "But of the day and that hour knoweth no man, no, not the angels which are in heaven, neither the Son, but the father."

He may come before this hour is over. He may not come for another hundred years. But here is the main thought: Are you ready for his coming?

2. But the World Is Full of Signs Which Point Toward That Great Day

"Coming events cast their shadows before." There are shadows all over the world today telling us that the end of the age is coming, and that the Lord will soon be back. Matthew 24:6-7: "And ye shall hear of wars and rumours of wars: see that ye be not troubled: for all these things must come to pass, but the end is not yet. For nations shall rise against nation, and kingdom against kingdom; and there shall be famines, and pestilences, and earthquakes, in divers places." This picture is certainly true today, isn't it? We are no longer fighting against Germany and Japan, but the world is still filled with "wars and rumours of wars."

The greatest war and the greatest famine and the greatest pestilence and the greatest earthquake the world has ever known up until that time occurred between 1912 and 1922. In 1939 a greater war began, at greater cost and with greater slaughter than ever before. These things have been with us always but never in the superlative degree in which we see them today. Yet these are just the "beginnings of sorrow."

We see next the persecution of the Jews. Matthew 24:9: "Then shall they deliver you up to be afflicted, and shall kill you: and ye shall be hated of all nations for my name's sake." This is a true picture of the Jews in recent years. Millions of them have been killed and driven from their homes. Today their lot is worse than ever. But these are just shadows of coming events. The Jew is the big sign of the end of the age; he is God's timetable. Jeremiah prophesied that before the end comes. they will return to their own land. In the Zionist Movement we have seen millions of them go back to Palestine. Many others are going when the way opens up for them.

We see next the increase of knowledge spoken of by Daniel. The world has advanced more in science and worldly wisdom in the last hundred years than it did in all the years which had gone into the tomb of time before this period.

Next, we see the coming of false prophets as spoken of in the twenty-fourth chapter of Matthew. Several men in the past few years have risen up in various countries and have said, "I am the Messiah." This is another sign that the true Christ must soon come.

One sure sign that Christ is coming soon is that of the great apostasy or falling away from religious truth. Paul describes this period in 2 Timothy 3:1-5. We are now in the midst of the perilous times which he talked about. Men everywhere are leaving the truth as it is in Christ Jesus. Modernism is flowing over the world like a mighty flood. The Bible has been kicked out of many churches and many sermons. Many of the prominent religious leaders of today don't believe in the deity of Christ, in atonement through the blood, in sin and hell. They laugh at the mention of the second coming. No wonder many churches are dead! No wonder they have lost their influence and power! Christ crucified is no longer preached from scores of our pulpits.

These are just a few of the signs of his coming. In this message there is not space to discuss these things in detail. What will happen between now and his coming? There is nothing left to happen—all the prophecies have been fulfilled. Soon the church will be complete, and Christ shall come again.

IV. WHAT ARE THE RESULTS OF HIS COMING?

What will happen to the people who are here, both the living and the dead? There are four groups to be dealt with:

1. The Dead in Christ Shall Rise First

The bodies of all those who died trusting Jesus will wing their way upward to meet him in the air.

2. The Living Christians Will Be Snatched Up to Meet Him in the Air

"Then we which are alive and remain shall be caught up together with them in the clouds to meet the Lord in the air." You need have no fear of his coming if you are living for him—he will take you up to meet him.

3. The Lost Dead Will Remain in Their Graves for a Thousand Years Longer

Revelation 20:5: "But the rest of the dead lived not again until the thousand years were finished." There are two resurrections from the dead—the resurrection of Christians, when Jesus comes in the air, and the resurrection of the lost, which will happen a thousand years later.

4. The Lost Living Ones Will Be Left to Face the Great Tribulation

It would take hours to tell of all the horrors of that period which is called the great tribulation. The Bible tells us that if those days were not shortened, human flesh would not be able to stand it.

Now this covers the disposal of these four groups. The dead Christians shall rise up to meet him, and the living Christians shall be caught up with him in the air. The dead sinners will remain in their graves a thousand years, and the living sinners will be left to face the great tribulation.

V. The Blessings Which His Coming Will Bring to Christians

1. We Will Be Taken Out of This World

The great tribulation is coming; the world will go through a tragic period of suffering. Our Lord will graciously take us out of the world before this experience. In his mercy he will save us from it all.

2. We Will Be Transformed

We are told in 2 Corinthians that we will be changed in the twinkling of an eye. Our vile bodies will be made just like his own glorious body. Sin and suffering and pain will be gone, and poor sinners at last will be like the stainless Son of God.

3. His Coming Brings Reunion with Our Loved Ones

We have wept at the bedside of those whom we loved. We have kissed them good-by. Our tears have flowed as we looked into the casket. We have gone home to find the vacant chair and to long for the touch of a vanished hand; but through our tears we have been able to say, "We will see them again." Yes, we will see our loved ones when Jesus comes. By his own power he will lift us up and then we will be reunited forever with those "whom we have loved long since and lost a while."

4. His Coming Brings Our Best Friend to Us

We try to live close to Jesus, but something is always between us and him. In that day we shall see him face to face. The best blessing will not be the robe or the crown or the mansion, but the sight which we shall have of our blessed Saviour. Surely we want to see him, we want to fall at his feet. We want to tell him how much we appreciate his death on the cross. We want to thank him for all that he has done, and, most of all, for taking us home to heaven.

5. His Coming Will Bring Us into the Sweetest and Highest Service

All of our human limitations will be removed, and we will serve him perfectly day and night. If we are faithful to him here, we will reign with him forever and ever.

VI. Lessons to Be Learned from the Fact of His Coming

1. We Must Be Ready

"And the door was shut." It is tragic to think of many who are going to be left behind. There is only one way to get ready, and that is to give your heart to Jesus Christ today.

On a certain morning Napoleon was slated to review his prize guard. These soldiers were many, many miles away, but they marched through the rain and the mud and arrived at their destination after midnight. They spent the rest of the night cleaning their uniforms. The next morning, when the emperor reviewed them, their uniforms were spotless. The heart of Napoleon was touched, and he said to them: "I am proud of you men. You stayed up all night long in order to get ready to meet your Emperor." Oh, our garments are stained with sin, but we can be ready to meet him. If we will come to him, he will wash us white as snow in his own blood.

2. We Must Be Watching

Matthew 24:42: "Watch therefore, for ye know not what hour your Lord doth come." Our hands should be busy with his work, but our eyes should be looking upward. One day I saw this motto on a piece of stationery, "Keep looking up." Your watching for Jesus does not keep you from being busy; it makes you become even more active in his service.

3. We Must Be Diligent in Service

We are to occupy until he comes. First Corinthians 1:7: "So that ye come behind in no gift; waiting for the coming of our Lord Jesus Christ." Someone said to John Wesley one day, "What would you do if you knew Jesus were coming tomorrow?" He then outlined his schedule for the coming day, and his friend said, "Why, that is just what you are going to do tomorrow." "Yes," said Mr. Wesley, "I live every day as if I knew that he were coming that day."

4. We Must Be Faithful

"Be thou faithful unto death, and I will give thee a crown of life." The city of Pompeii was completely covered by the lava and the brimstone which flowed from Mount Vesuvius. In recent years various groups of scientists have been digging down into the ruins of this ancient city. One group found a sentry still on duty at his post, which faced toward the center of the city. They found the bones of others in such positions that they knew these were running away from the city. But this sentry was standing and doing his duty. He seemed to be saying, "My master put me here and, whatever happens, I am going to be faithful to him."

Oh, friends, Jesus put us here to serve him and to make him known to the world! Let us say, "I don't know when he is coming, but I want him to find me faithful. Whatever happens, I am going to be faithful to my Master."

John, the beloved, stood yonder upon the Isle of Patmos. Jesus came and said to him, "Behold, I come quickly!" The old saint of God looked up in longing and cried out, "Even so, come, Lord Jesus." We would say today from the depths of our hearts, "Even so, come, Lord Jesus"; take us out of this world of sin and trouble and take us to thyself. If he should come, would you be ready? Get ready, for the Bridegroom cometh!

11

HELL, THE EVERLASTING HOME OF THE LOST

And in hell he lift up his eyes, being in torments, and seeth Abraham afar off, and Lazarus in his bosom.—Luke 16:23.

A certain minister had just finished preaching a strong Bible sermon on hell. A man from the congregation said to him later, "Don't you know that the more up-to-date preachers have taken hell out of the Bible?" The preacher replied, "They may have done that, but here is the trouble: they haven't destroyed the place." Jonathan Edwards preached his mighty sermon on "The Sinner in the Hands of an Angry God" many, many times. It is said that when he preached this sermon, men would grip the backs of the pews in order to keep from falling down into the pits of hell. Now hell is just as hot as it was when Jonathan Edwards preached about it, and it is just as real as it was when Jesus talked about it.

The doctrine of hell isn't a popular doctrine—I would much rather preach on heaven; but I would be preaching only a half gospel if I left hell out. We do not like to talk about hell, neither do we like to talk about murder, poverty, sickness, or death, but these things are facts just the same. Though we do not like to think about it, we must face the fact of sin and its punishment. We must realize that men do sin in this world—that there is a judgment to come, and that God has reserved punishment for sinners in another world.

114

I. There Is a Hell

1. The Bible Teaches It

The Bible is our sole authority. We are absolutely dependent upon it for our knowledge of the future life. Men have written great books, but God has written the one Book which tells us about the life that is to come. Those teachings on the subject of hell are very plain. Psalm 9:17: "The wicked shall be turned into hell, and all the nations that forget God." Daniel 12:2: "And many of them that sleep in the dust of the earth shall awake, some to everlasting life, and some to shame and everlasting contempt." Matthew 25:46: "And these shall go away into everlasting punishment: but the righteous into life eternal." Revelation 20:15: "And whosoever was not found written in the book of life was cast into the lake of fire."

But someone says, "I believe in heaven, but I do not believe in hell." You ask him the question, "Why do you believe in heaven?" and he says, "I read about it in the Bible. Jesus told us that he was going to prepare a wonderful place where we might life forever." Well, the same Bible which tells us about heaven also tells us about hell—and the Bible says much more about hell than it does about heaven. We must believe the Bible. Hell is certain, and we do wrong when we hide this fact from anyone.

If I saw you racing sixty miles an hour toward an open pit and you knew nothing of this danger, it would be my duty to warn you of the impending disaster. Let me say to you that hell lies out before all who reject Christ as Saviour. It is certainly the duty of the preacher, therefore, to warn you of the wrath which is to come.

2. Human Logic Demands It

When one man murders another, we say about the murderer, "That man should suffer; he doesn't deserve to enjoy the peace and happiness which good men deserve." Men are eternal criminals against God. They have sinned and broken his law. Logic says that they must be punished. We read that "Judas went to his own place." God does have a place for those who have trampled his Son underfoot. He has a penitentiary for criminals—he has a prison for sinners. But someone will say, "God is too good to send a man to hell." God does love every man, but his love doesn't cover up his justice. He gives a sinner every chance. He loves him and gives his Son to die for him and constantly pleads with the sinner to give his heart to Christ. If, after all this, a man is damned, it is not God's fault; it is the fault of the sinner. God is love, but God is just, also.

There are two places for the soul of man. It is unthinkable that murderers, thieves, liars, and adulterers will go to heaven. Heaven would become hell if it were filled with such people. Logic, therefore, demands that there shall be some place where the evil are punished. The name of this place of punishment is hell.

II. What Kind of Place Is Hell?

1. Hell Is a Place of Separation

"Depart from me, ye cursed." Hell means separation from God's presence and from God's blessings. Hell means separation from our loved ones who are at home with God.

Here is a soul who has been brought to judgment. He has lived in sin. He has spurned his father's prayers and his mother's tears. He has scorned every invitation to his heart. He has said, "I will live without God." Thus in the here and now he damns himself to receive the sentence at the final judgment: an eternity of separation from God.

2. Hell Is a Place of Suffering

Men suffer here, but this is nothing to compare with the sufferings of hell. For that is surely the most intense sort of suffering. Someone may ask the question: "Is there literal fire in hell?" We cannot answer that question, but Jesus uses sufficient language in describing the place. He talks about "the hell of fire," "the place where the fire is not quenched," "the furnace of fire," "the lake of fire." He tells about a man being "tormented in this flame." We have as much right to interpret this fire as being literal as we do of other references to fire in the Bible. The Bible speaks of the "fire on Elijah's altar," and we know that it was real fire. The Bible speaks of the bush which burned with fire, but was not consumed. We know that this was real fire. We cannot say, then, that hell isn't real fire; it is that or something worse.

You may say that the Bible descriptions of hell are just pictures. Well, the real thing is usually worse than the picture. We are not afraid of the picture of a storm, or of the picture of a forest fire, but we are afraid of the real thing, for it is much worse than the picture. If the Bible is simply giving us a picture of hell, surely then, hell, the real thing, must be much worse.

3. Hell Is a Place of Eternal Suffering

It would not be so bad if we had hope that the suffering some day would end, but it is eternal and everlasting. When you think of the body being consumed in hell and realize that this suffering never ends, we come to know what a terrible place, indeed, it must be. Death is a monster on earth, but men would welcome it as an angel in hell. If death could go down into hell and relieve the suffering of those who are there, the damned would rejoice. But death never comes to put an end to existence in hell.

We cannot do without hope in this world; yet there is no hope in hell. It is suffering, suffering, suffering, suffering, and no hope of escape. When you are sick, you hope that you will soon be better. When business is bad, you hope that it will soon improve. When you are in debt, you hope that you will soon be relieved of this debt. In this world we can always hope for something better, but there is no hope for those who go down to hell. "Forever lost" is written upon every chain of hell and blazes in every fire of that lost region.

Sixteen miles from Atlanta, Stone Mountain lifts its head toward the sky. This mountain is certainly a modern wonder of the world. There isn't another mountain within twenty-five miles, but this great solid mass of stone has stood there through the years attracting the interest of millions of people. It is about three-fourths of a mile high and eight miles around the base, and is formed of solid granite.

Someone has used this story to illustrate the length of eternity: Suppose an eagle flew over this mountain every one hundred years and simply touched the top of the mountain with the tip of his wing. He would then go away and come back again at the end of another hundred years, tipping the mountain again with his wings. When through this process the eagle had worn the mountain down level to the ground about it, eternity would have just begun. Think, then, about how terrible it will be to spend all that eternity in hell. Oh, the suffering of hell!

4. Hell Is a Place of the Lowest Associations

Revelation 21:8: "But the fearful, and unbelieving, and the abominable, and murders, and whoremongers, and sorcerers, and idolaters, and all liars, shall have their part in the lake which burneth with fire and brimstone: which is the second death."

But someone will say, "I am not a bad sinner; I do not belong in that crowd." You will notice, however, that this passage includes the "unbelievers." They may be good people, but if they haven't believed in Jesus Christ, they will be just as much lost as the murderers and whoremongers.

Some years ago, up in Virginia, a preacher was holding a revival meeting. A certain young lady, who wasn't a Christian, walked down the street one night after the service with her father and with the preacher. The preacher had sought in vain to win her to Christ. As they walked along, they passed by a carnival and saw a group of drunken women. The sight was replusive. Suddenly the preacher said to the young woman, "How would you like to live with them?" In amazement the young woman said, "What do you mean?" And the preacher said, "If you do not give your heart to Christ, you will have to live with them, not in this world, but through all eternity." The young woman saw the point, and immediately left her sin and gave herself to Christ. Yes, hell is a place of the lowest associations.

5. Hell Is the Place Where Men Reap the Harvest of Their Sinful Influence

"There will be weeping and gnashing of teeth." Certainly men will gnash their teeth as they reap the harvest of their sinful years. One man will gnash his teeth at a companion, saying, "You led me to this place! You told me to take my first drink." And the other one will say in reply, "Yes, but you made me even worse than I was by your influence." A son will turn to his father and, as he gnashes his teeth, he will cry out: "Father, you led me here! You had no time for the church. You left Christ out of your life. I followed you and went down into sin, and I am here today because of you." A daughter will turn upon her mother and, as she gnashes her teeth, she will say: "Mother, you led me to this place! You gave all your time to the world. You had no time for Christ. I followed you, and now I am lost because of it."

Oh, yes, my friends, each of us has an influence. We lift people up or we cast them down. We take them to heaven or we take them to hell. This thought ought to sober us and make us live rightly before God and before those who are looking to us on every side. In hell you reap the harvest of sinful influence.

6. Hell Is a Place of Memory

Abraham said to the rich man in hell, "Son, remember." And this man did remember. And the memory of his misspent life simply added fuel to the fires of hell. If you go to hell, you will remember some things, also. You will remember the gospel sermons that you heard. You will remember your mother's prayers. You will remember the personal words which were spoken to you by your friends. You will remember every time you came to church. You will remember how the invitations were given, and how you turned Christ down and did not come to him. Yes, you will remember, but it will be too late. You will be beyond redemption. You will be shut up in hell forever with your memory.

III. WHO GOES TO HELL?

1. Lost Sinners Go to Hell

"The soul that sinneth, it shall die." "The wages of sin is death." God has never changed these eternal statements. God is against sin, and sin is against God, and it must be punished.

2. The Unbelievers Go to Hell

One man will say, "I don't believe in Christ. He is not my Saviour, but I am living a good life." Yes, but the Bible tells us that the unbelievers will have their part in the lake of fire. "He that believeth not is condemned already." You can go your way without Christ now, but some day you will believe in him and it will be too late.

3. The Rejectors of Christ Go to Hell

To trample God's only begotten Son underfoot is the greatest sin that a man can commit. But you say, "I do not drink—I do not curse—I have never committed adultery." But this is the sin that damns you: You have rejected Christ as your Saviour. If your name isn't written in the Lamb's book of life, you will be cast into the lake of fire. You may go through life saying, "I am too busy with this world—I have no time for Christ." At last you will have time to die, and you will wake up in hell because you have rejected the only way of salvation.

IV. WHEN DOES HELL BEGIN?

1. Conscious Suffering of the Soul Begins at Death

The bodies of the wicked are not raised until a thousand years after the coming of Christ, but the suffering of the soul begins at death. However, this is the suffering which comes before the judgment of the great white throne and isn't the full measure of the suffering which the lost soul will later be forced to endure.

2. The Suffering of the Body Begins at the Judgment of the Great White Throne

The Bible teaches that at the resurrection of the wicked dead, the soul and body will come together, face the judgment of the great white throne, and then be cast into hell. Revelation 20:13: "And the sea gave up the dead which were in it; and death and hell delivered up the dead which were in them: and they were judged every man according to their works."

But someone says, "Why do we have the judgment of the great white throne if suffering begins with the soul at death?" When a lost man dies, his soul goes to the place of suffering. At the great white throne judgment, his soul and body (reunited) will face the throne. All the works of life will be over, and the man will be judged according to the works done. The sinner is already lost because he rejected Christ in this world, but his suffering will be determined by the evil works done here in the body.

The Bible seems to teach that there will be degrees of suffering in hell. "For unto whomsoever much is given, of him shall much be required." Jesus tells us in the parable of the steward that the one who knew the Lord's will and did it not would be beaten with many stripes, but the one who knew not his will and committed things worthy of stripes should be beaten with few stripes.

When a man dies, his work isn't done, and the man must be judged according to his works. For instance, a certain man writes a book. This man dies, but after his death this book still does an evil work, leading men away from Christ. At death he cannot be judged according to his works, because his works are not yet finished. But when he faces the great white throne, all the results will be in, and he will be judged acording to the finished work.

So we see that, while suffering begins at death, this isn't the full measure of suffering. At the judgment all works will be complete, and lost men will then suffer according to those works. We must remember, then, that a man goes to hell because he rejects Christ, and he suffers in hell according to the evil works done as an unbeliever.

V. How to Escape Hell

1. Turn from Your Sins

Don't say that God sends you to hell—it is your own sin which does this. You must turn away from your sin, for God is a holy God, and you cannot carry your sin up to heaven with you. If you hold to your sin, you will go down to hell with it, and throughout all eternity sin will mock you, crying out, "Ah, ha! It was sweet to sin while you were living, but you will pay for it now."

Why did the rich man go to hell? It was because he did not repent. He might have been a good church member, but he did not repent of his sins. Listen to him as he cries out, "Tell my brothers to repent so they will not come to this place." That is why anyone goes to hell. The only way to escape hell and get to heaven is to repent of your sin.

Some lost man may knock at the door of heaven, crying out, "Let me in! Let me in!" The question will come back, "By what right do you expect to enter heaven?" And the man will say, "My mother is in there—she loved me and prayed for me." But the answer will come back, "That doesn't matter now; you did not pray for yourself; you did not trust Christ." "But," the man will cry out, "my father is there. He was a good man—he told me about Christ." And the answer will come back, "Yes, he is here, but you cannot get in, because you rejected Christ —you did not heed the warnings of your father." The prayers of your loved ones may be piled up to the stars for you, but this will not get you into heaven unless you repent of your sin and come to the Saviour.

A godly woman dreamed that she stood near the great judgment throne. She was on one side, and her children were on the other side. The children cried out, "Mother, must we part?" And she said, "If it were possible, I would take you with me." But just then an angel touched her and she was transformed and changed in every way. Having now the mind of Christ, she said to her children, "I told you about the Lord. I tried to bring you to trust him, but you have scorned the ways of God and gone down into sin, and all that I can say now is 'Amen' to your condemnation." she had been made supernatural. Now she saw that God's ways were just and right. So when the voice of God rang out, "Depart from me," the voice of the mother beside the throne uttered a sincere "Amen." It is only right that those who reject Christ should go to hell. You must repent to escape this penalty.

2. You Must Turn to Jesus

Now this is repentance: to turn from sin in godly sorrow and to turn to Jesus in saving faith. Your works will not keep you out of hell. Your goodness will not keep you out of hell. "By grace are ye saved through faith."

Charles H. Spurgeon never tired of telling the story of how he was saved. He had been trying to save himself by his own works. Then one rainy Sunday morning he wandered into a little chapel and sat down with the few worshipers who were there. That morning the minister preached on the text, "Look unto me, all ye ends of the earth, and be ye saved." At the close of his sermon, he pointed his long, bony finger at young Spurgeon and said, "Look! Look unto him, young man! Look unto Jesus, and you will be saved." That morning Spurgeon looked unto Jesus and was gloriously and wondrously saved. Sinner, that is all you need to do— just look. Look to Jesus—look to him in saving faith. Look away from your sins and look to Jesus. Then you will be rejoicing that your name has been written in the Lamb's book of life.

In the old days a schoolmaster came to a certain home and said to the father, "Where is your boy?" The father investigated and learned that the boy had been playing "hooky." After a talk with his father, the boy said, "God helping me, I will never do it again." The father forgave him; but the law of nature says that sin must be punished. So the father sent the boy to the dark garret room to sleep for the next several nights. The first night the father and mother could not rest. The mother sat by the fireside sewing, and the father tried to read, but their hearts were upstairs in the darkness with that boy. They went to bed, but they could not sleep. They heard the clock chime eleven, and then twelve, and then one. Finally the father could stand it no longer; so he took his pillow and went up to the dark garret room to sleep with the boy. He lay down by the boy, drew him close to his heart and finally went to sleep, bearing the boy's puunishment along with him. He did this every night that the boy was supposed to stay in the garret room. The father was innocent, but he suffered in order to put the boy right.

Oh, my friends, Jesus came to our garret room of sin and suffered for us. He did more than any father can ever do; he took our place and paid the debt that we owed. God help us to accept him, and thus shall we escape hell, the everlasting home of the lost.

12

HEAVEN, THE LAND OF NO TEARS

And God shall wipe away all tears from their eyes; and
there shall be no more death, neither sorrow, nor crying,
neither shall there be any more pain: for the former things
are passed away.—REVELATION 21:4.

In these little lives of ours we must think of two worlds.
We commit spiritual suicide if we live for this world only
and think nothing of the world which is to come. Every
sensible man knows that there is another land and another
life, and every sensible man wants to live that life in the
best possible way. Let us today contrast these two
worlds—the land in which we now live, which is the land
of tears, and God's heaven, which is the land of no tears.
Jesus told us that he was going to prepare a place for us
where we might live forever with him. And while John
was on the isle of Patmos, God pulled back the curtain of
eternity and gave him the privilege of looking upon the
glories of our future home. Inspired and illumined by
the Spirit of God, John wrote for us a vivid description
of heaven in the book of Revelation.

I. THIS EARTH IS THE LAND OF TEARS

This world is full of tears. We find them at every
corner and every turn of the road. The sun might shine
for us a little while, but soon the sun is gone, the shadows
gather round us, and we are bound to shed our bitter
tears.

1. There Are the Tears of Disappointment

Things may look bright for us for a while, but then
some blinding disappointment comes to rob us of our

peace and to bring sorrow to our hearts. Moses spent his entire life with one great goal in view. It was his supreme ambition to take the children of Israel into the Land of Promise. Just when it seemed that he was going to realize the fulfilment of his dreams, the disappointment came. God took him up on a high mountain and gave him the first view of the land which was "flowing with milk and honey." How his heart must have thrilled as he looked into Canaan with the hope that soon he would lead the children of Israel into their new home! Then God said to him: "Moses, because of your disobedience, you will not be able to go into the Land of Promise. Your successor will lead Israel into its new home." As we see the tears course down the cheeks of the old patriarch, we realize that he was shedding the tears of disappointment.

2. There Are the Tears of Our Shattered Dreams

We build our castles in the air only to see them come crashing down to the earth. We dream our bright dreams which never come true. We have high hopes which never materialize. We look forward to great days which never dawn for us.

In the slums of London there lived a poor man and woman who had an only son. They made many sacrifices in order to give this son a good education. They sent him through the grammar school, the high school, and the university. He was graduated from the university with high honors, majoring in chemistry, and on the day of his graduation he was given a position as chemist in a great chemical plant. With the first money that he made, he moved his parents out of the slums into a little rose-covered cottage on the edge of the city. Prospects like the rosy dawn gleamed forth for them, for their son had a splendid job. He loved them, and he was going to take care of them for the rest of their lives. And then one day there was an explosion in the chemical plant and the young man was made an invalid for life. Surely the little family must have shed the tears of shattered dreams.

3. There Are the Tears of Death

Darker than any corner in hell is that corner in which we stand when sorrow comes, and our loved ones have been taken away. We sit in sorrow at their funeral. We put them away from the sight of human eyes, and we come back home to find a vacant chair. We "long for the touch of a vanished hand, and the sound of a voice that is still." Certainly life seems empty, and our hearts are heavy as lead.

I catch the scent of orange blossoms, and I see a handsome young man and a beautiful young woman stand before the minister, plighting their troth until death parts them. The years pass by. A dear little baby girl comes to bless their union. One day the little child is sick. The parents call in the best doctors, but every effort is in vain. The little baby goes out to be with God, and the poor young father and mother fold their broken wings about each other and shed the tears of death. My mother died when I was a little boy, and even now I can see my father, a big strong man, walking up and down the long hall and crying out unto God. I can see my sister going to the bedside of my mother and crying out to a mother who could never come back to this earth. Our little family had been robbed of its sweetest human possession, and we were shedding the tears of death.

Yes, this old world is full of tears. But we thank God that there is a land where all tears are wiped away. I wish that I had the words of a flaming orator that I might paint such a picture upon the canvass of your imagination as to cause you to want to leave this sinful earth and soar away to be with God in heaven forever. Since I cannot do this, I will simply give you some simple facts about heaven.

II. Heaven Is the Land of No Tears

1. Heaven Is a Place

Jesus said, "I go to prepare a place for you"; and I get great comfort in taking Jesus at his word. Heaven is a prepared place for a prepared people. Christ has done his part—he has prepared the place and prepared the way to that place. Are you prepared for heaven? Are you walking in the way which Christ has made? John stood upon the isle of Patmos and saw a great company of people in heaven. The angel said to him, "These are they which came out of the great tribulation, and have washed their robes, and made them white in the blood of the Lamb." Our robes are filthy with the sin of this old world, and they must be washed white in the blood of the Lamb if we are to enter heaven. Yes, heaven is a prepared place for a prepared people.

2. Heaven Is a Perfect Place

Jesus was a carpenter before he entered the ministry, and I know that he always did a good job and never charged too much. And when he went away to be the Architect of heaven, I am sure that he went away to build a perfect place for you and me.

Heaven is spoken of as a city twelve thousand furlongs square. This means that heaven would contain about fifteen hundred square miles. Someone has figured that if you started at Jacksonville, Florida, drawing a line northward to New York City, then westward to St. Paul Minnesota, then southward to Galveston, Texas, then eastward to Jacksonville, Florida, you would have an area just about the size of heaven. Oh, my friends, heaven must be bigger and finer than that. These are poor human figures, and we cannot measure heaven in these terms. Its a wonderful place, too, for we are told that the walls are of jasper, and that every gate is a separate pearl. A string of pearls in this world is worth thousands of dollars, and any woman would be happy to possess some genuine pearls. But in that day we shall enter a gate of pearl, and it shall have very little attraction for us, for we will all be on the way to gaze into the face of him who was himself the Pearl of great price. We are told also, that the streets will be paved with gold. Men will do anything in this world for gold. They will rob, and cheat, and even kill for gold. Thank God at last, when we get to heaven, gold will be under our feet, and we shall worship it no longer, but we shall forever praise and adore the Lamb which was slain.

3. Heaven Is a Place Where Many People Will Be

There are some who are so selfish that they think you cannot get to heaven unless you belong to their church and believe just exactly as they do. I believe that there will be many people in heaven. God is a great God. He has prepared a great salvation, and surely he has a great heaven waiting for us.

Some people tell us that there will be only one hundred forty-four thousand people in heaven. John did mention that number, but then he said that he looked again and that he saw a great multitude which no man could number of every nation and kindred and people and tongue. If the great mathematicians of the world were to try to number this multitude, they would reel and stagger in the face of such stupendous figures. They are going to be the best people—those with all the sin and evil of life washed away from their hearts. I want to be there, too, don't you?

4. Heaven Is a Permanent City

Hebrews 13:14: "For here we have no continuing city, but we seek one to come." Rome, Athens, Carthage, Sparta—these ancient cities have either been destroyed or have lost their former glory. Babylon, the great city of Old Testament times, once had a population of two millions, but now snakes and lizards crawl across its ruins. It is true that we have no continuing city. Today we have New York, Chicago, London, Washington, and the other great cities, but there is no permanent city on this earth. These will soon be gone. Thank God, the Holy City, the New Jerusalem, will abide forever and ever. It is a permanent city.

5. Heaven Is a City of Perfect Residences

We are contented down here in this world with some small place that we can call our own, but in that world we will have a mansion. Why should we then be so particular about amassing a fortune in this world when we have everything good waiting for us in the other world?

> A tent or a cottage, why should I care?
> They're building a palace for me over there.
> Though exiled from home, yet still may I sing
> All glory to God, I'm a child of the King.

Henry van Dyke tells us a story of a rich man who sat down on Christmas Eve to count his possessions. Becoming a bit weary, he put his head down upon the library table and went to sleep. He dreamed that he was in heaven walking down the streets with the recording angel. They went down one street which was filled with lovely and pretentious homes. Soon the man stopped in front of a beautiful residence and said to the recording angel, "Who is so fortunate even in heaven as to be able to have such a home as this?" The recording angel looked in his book and said to the man, "This home belongs to your gardener." The rich man said: "Certainly you folks have made a mistake. This man lived in a very poor cottage on my estate. This cannot be his home." But the angel answered, "We make no mistakes in heaven." They resumed their walk, and soon turned down a very small street. Each home was smaller and less pretentious than the one before it. Soon the man stopped in front of a very small house and laughingly said, "Who is so unfortunate even in heaven as to be forced to live in a small place like this?" The recording angel looked in his book and said to the man, "Sir, this is your home." "I know you have made a mistake now," said the man, "Down in the world I lived in the finest houses money could buy. I had a winter home and a summer home, a country home and a town home. This cannot be my home." "It is your home," said the angel. "We make no mistakes in heaven. This home has been built out of the material that you sent up here from the earth."

How much treasure are you laying up in heaven? The reward which comes to you there is dependent upon the service which you give to Christ here.

6. Heaven Is a Place of Perfect Music

All of us love music; it thrills our souls and lifts us up to God. When Billy Sunday was in the zenith of his power, he would have choirs composed sometimes of two thousand voices. What a thrill it was to hear Homer Rodeheaver lead these great choirs in song! Do you know how big the choir will be in heaven? In Revelation 5:11 we are told that the choir will consist of one hundred million voices—everybody in perfect harmony— everybody singing praises to the Lamb that was slain.

7. Heaven Is a Place of Perfect Knowledge

"Now I know in part; but then shall I know even as also I am known." We wonder why God allows sin to come into the world to break our hearts and blast our hopes. We wonder why a precious, useful loved one is taken away and someone who is worth very little is left in the world. We shall never know the answer in this world, but in the golden glow of that better land we shall sit down by the side of the Lord Jesus and he will explain it all to us. We will learn then that these things which seem hard are simply blessings in disguise. In that day there will be no secrets between us and God. "Now we see through a glass, darkly, but then face to face."

8. Heaven Is a Place of Perfect Service

The most miserable people in the world are those who are idle. They fill the jails and the asylums. Heaven is a place of perfect service. There will be only one occupation for those who inhabit hell: they will spend eternity in suffering, brooding over what might have been if they had only given their hearts to Christ. But those who go to heaven will bring their talents home to Jesus. He will say to them, "Well done," and will set them to work in some place of perfect service.

> When earth's last picture is painted and the tubes are twisted and dried,
> When the oldest colours have faded, and the youngest critic has died,
> We shall rest, and, faith, we shall need it—lie down for an aeon or two,
> Till the Master of All Good Workmen shall put us to work anew!
> And those that were good will be happy; they shall sit in a golden chair;
> They shall splash at a ten-league canvas with brushes of comet's hair;

They shall find real saints to draw from—Magdalene,
  Peter and Paul;
They shall work for an age at a sitting and never be
  tired at all.
And only the Master shall praise us, and only the
  Master shall blame;
And no one shall work for money, and no one shall
  work for fame;
But each for the joy of working, and each, in his
  separate star,
Shall paint the Thing as he sees It for the God of
  Things as they are!

                                        —Rudyard Kipling

9. Heaven Is a Perfect Home

Home is the dearest spot on earth, but you will never
find one that is perfect. We live happily with our loved
ones about us, but one day a son goes away to another
state to seek his fortune, or a daughter marries and goes
to another part of the country. Our homes are thus
broken up. We go to our family reunions once a year,
and we miss those who gladdened our hearts in other
days. Yes, our homes are often broken up down here,
but they will never be broken up in heaven. In the
vocabulary of God there is no such word as "good-by."
Those who love God never part for the last time.

There was a time when I had no interest in Daytona
Beach, Florida. But one day my only sister moved to
that city, and now I am deeply interested in it because
I have a loved one there. We go along without any
thought of heaven until one day one of our loved ones
goes over to the Eternal City. We are then linked to the
throne of God by the silver cord of love and memory.
I believe that we shall know our loved ones in heaven,
also. The disciples knew Moses and Elijah when they
came back to talk to Jesus on the Mount of Transfigura-
tion. Someone said to Dwight L. Moody, "Do you think
we will know each other in heaven?" And the great

preacher replied, "Certainly I do. Surely we will have just as much sense there as we have here."

10. Heaven Is a Place of Perfect Rest

We get mighty tired down here. Often our bodies are racked with pain, and we are daily suffering the anguish of the flesh. But in that day we shall find perfect rest, and suffering and sorrow shall flee away. We are told in Philippians 3:21 that Christ at his coming shall change our vile bodies and make them like unto his own glorious body.

I wonder if God doesn't permit us to suffer sometimes in order that we might better appreciate heaven. If the sun shone every day and never a cloud filled the sky, we would not appreciate the sunshine. Heaven will be more wonderful to us because we have suffered here in this world. The apostle Paul suffered more than any other man has ever suffered for the sake of Christ, and he was able to say, "For I reckon that the sufferings of this present time are not worthy to be compared with the glory which shall be revealed in us" (Romans 8:18); and "For our light affliction, which is but for a moment, worketh for us a far more exceeding eternal weight of glory" (2 Corinthians 4:17).

Even Jesus looked forward to heaven, "for the joy that was set before him endured the cross, despising the shame, and is set down at the right hand of the throne of God." When he sees the great throng which enters heaven, he shall "see of the travail of his soul, and shall be satisfied." Will you be in that great throng when the saints go marching in?

11. Heaven Is a Place Where Jesus Is

If the golden streets, the crown, and the robe were all of heaven, it would not be worth the struggle; but heaven is a place where we are going to see Jesus. Just one glimpse of his face is worth giving up everything in order that we might reach heaven and see him. There are many we are anxious to see in heaven. Maybe you want to see that father—that mother—that loved one who left you years ago. But first of all surely you will want to see Jesus, because he is the one who made heaven possible for us.

Pat was an Irishman and a great Christian. Some years ago he sailed across the ocean and came to a new home and a new task in America. On the voyage to America, his little boy died, and was buried at sea. After he had been here a few months he received the message that his father had died back in Ireland. And yet one day, when someone asked him the question, "Pat, what are you going to do when you get to heaven?" he answered by saying, "I am going to spend the first five hundred years just a-looking at the Lord Jesus." He wanted to see that little baby again—he wanted to see his father again—but when the testing time came he said, "First of all I want to see Jesus."

John Jasper was a great Negro preacher of Richmond, Virginia. Both the white people and the Negroes crowded his church every Sunday to hear his mighty gospel messages. One day he was preaching about heaven, and when he came to the climax of his sermon, he was overcome by his emotion and could not proceed further. He motioned the people to leave the church as he started back toward his study door. But before he reached the door, his will asserted itself, and he came back and leaned over the pulpit and finished his message. He said to his congregation, "Some of dese days old John Jasper is gwine to die. He is gwine to go up to heaven and walk down the golden streets. An angel is gwine to come up and say, 'John Jasper, don' you want your robe what's done been washed white in de blood of de Lamb?' and I am going to say to him, 'Yes, Marse angel, I sho does want dat robe, but first of all I wants to see my Marse Jesus.'" Then he said, "I will go down the street and will meet anudder angel, and he will say, 'Look here, John Jasper, don' you want your crown which is bedecked wid so many jewels' cause of the souls you have won to Jesus?' and I'm gwine to say to him, 'Yes, mighty angel, I does want dat crown, but first of all I wants to find my Marse Jesus and fall down at his feet and thank him for saving such a sinner as I was!'" Surely everyone of us feels this same way.

Dr. Len G. Broughton was for some years pastor of the Baptist Tabernacle of Atlanta. In his congregation he had a fine young Christian man who was an usher in the church. This young man was quite sick, and Dr. Broughton went to see him. The young man knew that he could not live much longer, and he and his pastor talked about the heavenly city toward which he was going. As the young man talked about death and heaven, the tears welled up in his eyes. Dr. Broughton took a handkerchief from his pocket, reached over and wiped the tears from first one eye and then the other. The young man then smiled and, looking up into the preacher's face, he said, "The next time my tears are wiped away, they will be wiped away by the loving hand of my Heavenly Father."

My friends, don't you want to live in the land of no tears? Then you must make preparation for it. And there is only one way of preparation: give your heart to Jesus Christ, put your life in his hand, and he will take you safely at last to the land of no tears.